The HORSE in WAR

The HORSE in WAR

Edited by Michael Seth-Smith

NEW ENGLISH LIBRARY
TIMES MIRROR

Copy Editor: William J. Howell
Art Editor: Deborah Miles
Design: Nykola Stoakes

This edition published in 1979 by
New English Library Limited,
Barnard's Inn,
Holborn,
London EC1N 2JR,
England

© Text and illustrations copyright New
English Library Limited 1979

Set in 11/12 pt Times Roman by
Hunt Barnard Printing Ltd
Printed by Fratelli Spada, Ciampino,
Rome, Italy

450 03602 2

Introduction

Although the horse has carried man to war for more than three thousand years, it is only in modern times that cavalry have played an important part in achieving victory in battle. In previous centuries the horse was used by war lords and conquerors as a fast means of transport for their soldiers, for reconnaissance and for carrying messages and despatches. An early reference to men and horses appears in the Old Testament when an ambassador tells the King of Judah 'I pray thee, give pledges to my Lord, the King of Assyria, and I will deliver thee two thousand horses, if thou be able on thy part to set riders upon them', but it is doubtful if the horses were intended for use in battle. Even in the era of Genghis Khan the reason for mounting his soldiers on tough Mongolian ponies was to speed their movement across the desolate plains of Persia and Afghanistan rather than to inflict defeat upon the enemy.

King Richard III may have clamoured 'A horse, a horse, my kingdom for a horse' on Bosworth Field, and the Spaniards may have included war-horses aboard their Armada Fleet, but it was Oliver Cromwell who pioneered the calculated use of cavalry *en masse* as a battle-winning asset. He appreciated the advantage of keeping them in reserve until he considered the time ripe for the onslaught, with the consequent rout and annihilation of the opposing forces. Frederick the Great and Napoleon were also military geniuses who understood the vital importance of maintaining strict control of their cavalry on the field of battle and ordering them to charge at the critical moment.

During the past four centuries cavalry regiments have covered themselves with glory on many occasions, highlighted by their achievements at Waterloo, Omdurman where the young Winston Churchill so nearly lost his life, and at Balaclava, where the Charge of the Light Brigade has been immortalised by Lord Tennyson:

> When can their glory fade?
> O the wild charge they made!
>   All the world wonder'd

The death knell for cavalry, and for the horse in battle, was sounded in November 1917 at Cambrai when mechanised vehicles known as tanks were used for the first time – but despite this sentence of death nothing can ever detract from the vital role played by the horse in campaigns, battles and wars waged by man throughout history.

Michael Sett-Smith.

Contents

Napoleon at the Battle of Rivoli, 1797; from the painting in the Palace of Versailles. C. M. DIXON

The Wooden Horse of Troy

More than three thousand years ago the Greeks under Agamemnon, King of Mycenae, fought before the city of Troy for ten long years without avail. At last they became weary of their fruitless attacks, and were advised by the seer Calchas that they should stop attacking the walls and devise some stratagem whereby they could conquer the city.

Eventually the Greek hero Odysseus, always crafty, suggested that they should build a huge hollow wooden horse and leave it filled with men, while the remainder should sail away and hide behind the nearby island of Tenedos. The idea was accepted and the Greeks set to work with such a will that the horse was finished in three days.

The horse's belly was as large as a ship and on its lofty neck they fixed a crested mane of purple splashed with yellow gold. Its eyes were made of sea-green beryl with pupils of blood-red garnet. They put white teeth in its mouth and made an air vent, hidden in its mouth. They gave it pricked ears and a tail which flowed down to its heels, and its feet were made of bronze covered in tortoise-shell. They made a trap-door in the side for men to enter and fitted wheels so that it could be dragged along easily. Its bridle was purple and its bronze bit inlaid with ivory and silver. Upon the horse they put the inscription 'For their safe return home the Greeks dedicate this thank-offering to Athene.' The bravest of the Greeks, believed to have been between twenty-two and thirty-five soldiers, volunteered to enter the horse. Afterwards the Greeks burnt their tents and sailed away.

The Trojans came out from their walls and gathered about the horse. Some said that it should be dragged into the city, others that it should be burnt or thrown over the cliffs. Laocoön, the priest of Apollo, rushed down from the city with a large following of people and furiously urged them to put no trust in the horse, finishing his speech with the famous phrase, 'I fear the Greeks, especially when they bring gifts.' Whereupon he hurled his spear into the side of the horse and a sound like a groan issued from it.

But at that very moment the Trojans' attention was diverted by a shepherd dragging in Sinon, a relation of Odysseus, who said that he had incurred the wrath of Odysseus and must be sacrificed to ensure a safe passage home for the Greeks. Sinon also told the Trojans that if the horse were dragged into the temple of Athene in the city to replace the image of the goddess, which Odysseus had stolen some time before, Troy would never be captured and the Trojans would conquer Greece itself. The Trojans then began to drag the horse up into the city, breaking down the walls to do so. They strewed the way with flowers, while youths and maidens accompanied the horse with hymns.

Four times the horse stopped as they tried to drag it over the threshold of the temple, and each time the clash of arms sounded from within, but the Trojans in their frenzy, took no heed and took the horse into the sanctuary of Athene. The Trojans then devoted the evening to feasting and dancing. When night fell, most of the Trojans slept, overcome by

drunkenness and exhaustion. During the night Sinon lighted a fire, which was the agreed signal for the Greeks to return from Tenedos, and then went to the horse and helped the Greeks who were inside to descend by ropes and ladders. They fought their way to the gates and opened them to the returning Greeks. Amidst great carnage Troy fell. Only a few Trojans escaped, including Aeneas, the son of Anchises and Aphrodite who, as the founder of Latium, was also the founder of Rome.

Above: Detail from 'The Building of the Wooden Horse' by Tiepolo.
NATIONAL GALLERY, LONDON

Overleaf: Tiepolo's painting of the Wooden Horse being dragged into Troy.
NATIONAL GALLERY, LONDON

Giovanni Battista Tiepolo (1696-1770) has been described as 'the last of the great Venetian decorators'. He trained under Lazzarini, about whom little is known, but learned more by studying the works of Veronese and, among his contemporaries, of Ricci and Piazzetta. He had already painted the 'Sacrifice of Abraham' when he

was admitted to the Fraglia in 1717. Later in life he travelled widely until, in 1755, he was elected the first President of the Venetian Academy. Then, in 1762, he went to Madrid at the invitation of Charles III, with his sons and assistants, and spent four years painting the ceilings of the Palace. His last years in Spain were embittered by intrigues, and he died suddenly in Madrid.

How the Horse Saved the Chinese Empire

The Chinese were farmers at a very early period, unlike their nomadic neighbours to the north and west; they had horses, but they used them only for draught and burden. They did not ride at all before 300 BC, and it is not certain that their horses were ridable. This was true at the same time in northern Europe, where the little shaggy pony was always put between the shafts because it was simply too small to ride; in the case of the Chinese it was probably not so much the size of the horse that discouraged riding as its type and conformation.

It has been suggested that the Chinese harnessed Prjevalsky's horse, which was, and still is, the one type of horse to be a distinct species from *equus caballus*. It survives today in the wild state, carefully conserved, in small herds in some parts of Mongolia, and there are also a good many in zoos. Prjevalsky's is a clumsy-looking animal, with a big bearded head, an erect bootbrush mane, a very short neck, and an air of apathy. Chinese bronzes and sculptures of the early Han period portray, probably realistically, a horse very much like Prjevalsky's. It is no surprise that the Chinese did not attempt to ride this awkward creature.

When they did begin to ride, they did so on Mongolian ponies imported from the north to meet military requirements. The immensely long northern frontier of China was threatened by a new and ferocious enemy, the nomadic Hsiung-nu the Huns who had, by Chinese standards, the unbeatable mobility of good cavalry; it was only by cavalry that they could be contained. In adopting Hun strategy and horsemanship, the Chinese also, for riding, adopted Hun dress – long tunics and trousers quite unlike their normal garments. The imported Mongolian ponies were better than the old Prjevalsky's; but being the horses that the Huns themselves rode, they were

not good enough to enable the Chinese to beat the Huns. To do that, a completely new source of horses had to be found; it was found, in countries far to the west.

These were the countries – ancient Bactria and its neighbours to the west and south – that had been conquered

by Alexander the Great. Like most conquests of the ancient world, his were accomplished by superior cavalry. When the Greeks left, the descendants of their horses remained. *Bucephalus* himself, Alexander's own charger whom no one else could approach, was believed to be the ancestor of the very best horses in central Asia: as late as the thirteenth century AD Marco Polo heard of horses said to be descended from *Bucephalus* which had, like him, a distinctive blaze.

The Greeks had a large and lasting influence on the Asian empire they occupied, introducing lucerne as fodder for their horses, and also vines and viticulture. But the north-eastern part of their territory, like China itself, was threatened by the Huns, and about 135 BC they withdrew from Bactria south into the Punjab.

The horses that they left behind are generally accepted to be the celebrated Nisaean or Nesaean breed, which originated, according to the geographer Strabo, in Armenia or Media, in what is now far eastern Turkey, far southern Russia between the Black Sea and the Caspian, and far north-western Persia. This is speculative: Strabo did not record the tradition until about AD 1, and the Nisaean might have been known a good deal further east, on the other side of the Caspian.

The Nisaeans were a cross, it seems, of the big and rather coarse chariot- and saddle-horses of the Assyrians (who had the world's first effective cavalry, and the world's first hunting on horseback) with either the wonderful little horses of Libya or those of the Tigris and Euphrates delta; perhaps both. The descendant of the Libyan

Below: Bronze Flying Horse AD2 (Ch'in and Eastern Han Dynasty), a remarkable sculpture of a galloping horse balancing on a swallow and representing the tall western breed of 'supernatural' or 'celestial' horse first introduced into China in the first century BC by the Emperor Wu Ti.
PHOTOGRAPH BY CHRISTINA GASCOIGNE AND DEREK WITTY. ROBERT HARDING ASSOCIATES

13

was the Barb, of the Mesopotamian the Arab; both were brought from the southern steppes by the Hyksos, the nomadic 'shepherds' who conquered Asia Minor and the eastern Mediterranean about 1500 BC.

The best Greek horses – those which won the races at the Olympic and other games – were Libyan: but sporting Persian kings like Cyrus, who invented pigsticking and could ride down a fox or wild ass with a spear, had better and faster horses than the Greeks. The best racehorses of the Roman Empire were also Libyan; fragments found in Rome, pieces of ancient stonework built into a later wall, have been pieced together into a kind of Racing Calendar, an official list of winners of races in the Circus Maximus, with their places of origin. Almost all were Libyan.

But whereas the Greeks had a single breed of dainty little horse for all purposes, the Romans developed, in ascending order of size and strength, distinct racehorses, hunters, cavalry chargers and harness-horses. This they did by breeding Libyans to more substantial breeds like Turcomans. This is in effect what the Persians had done, the result was that King Cyrus had better horses than Xenophon ever saw at home in Greece, and the king's were Nisaeans.

It is relevant to note in this connection that Arab and Barb blood only became that of the Thoroughbred racehorse, a much taller and faster animal, after crossing with mares of less quality but more substance. It would be grotesque to equate the creation of the Nisaean with the creation of the Thoroughbred,

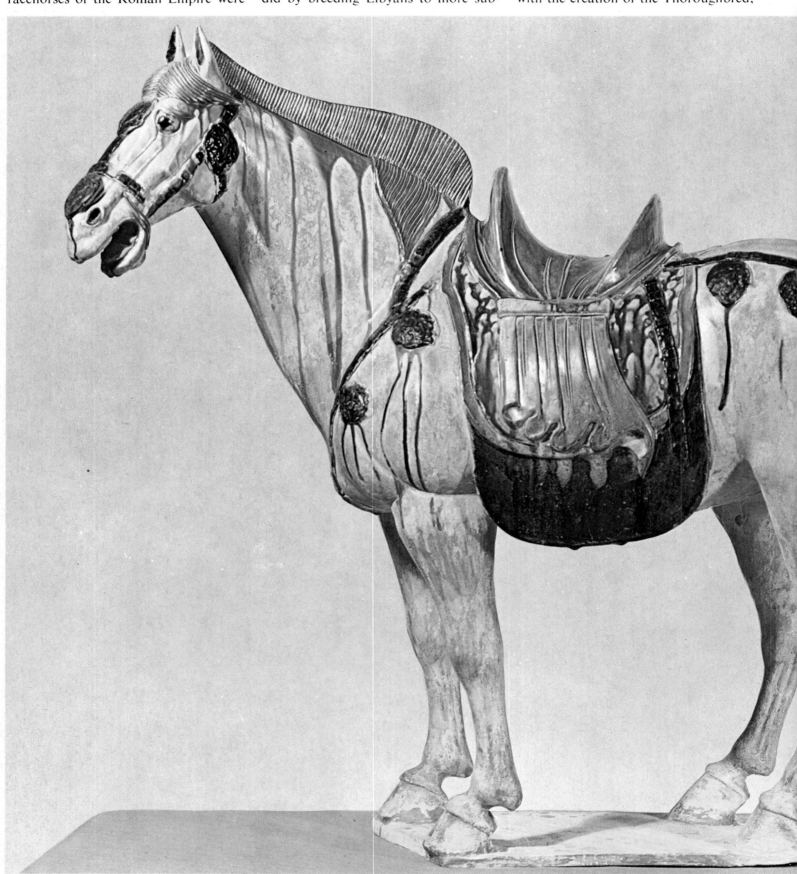

but it is not grotesque to make a cautious comparison: A more recent analogy is the production of heavyweight hunters (and today of eventers) by a first or second cross of Thoroughbred with Cleveland Bay. The Cleveland Bay itself, like the Norfolk Trotter and other class harness-horses of moderate size, was a Thoroughbred-Friesland cross. The Nisaean is the supreme example in the ancient world of this kind of breeding.

Within a decade of the Greek withdrawal from Bactria, the Chinese were beginning to open up trade-routes to

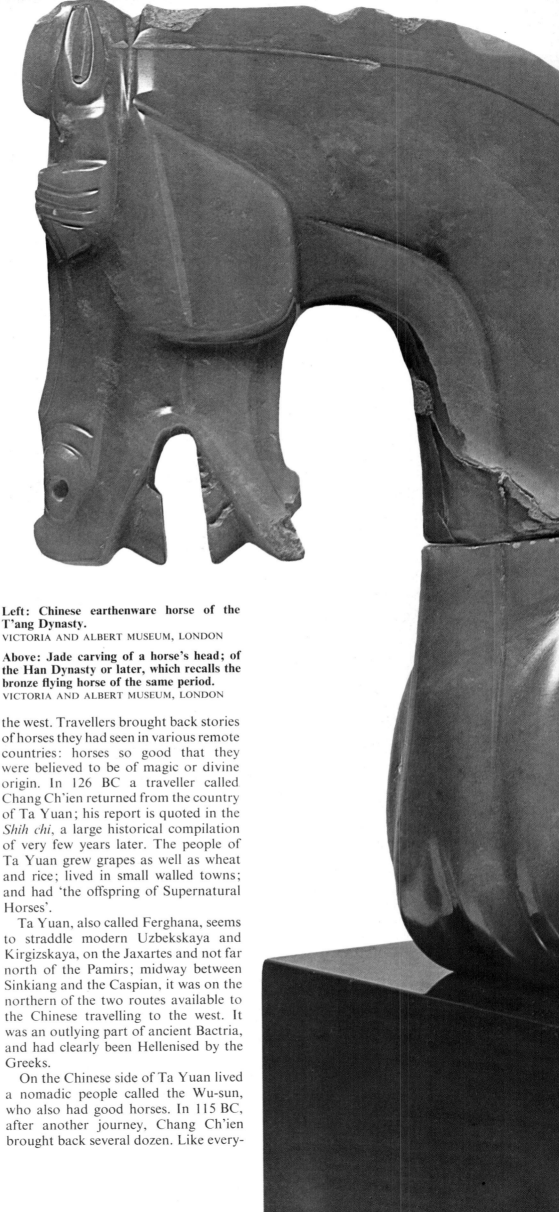

Left: Chinese earthenware horse of the T'ang Dynasty.
VICTORIA AND ALBERT MUSEUM, LONDON

Above: Jade carving of a horse's head; of the Han Dynasty or later, which recalls the bronze flying horse of the same period.
VICTORIA AND ALBERT MUSEUM, LONDON

the west. Travellers brought back stories of horses they had seen in various remote countries: horses so good that they were believed to be of magic or divine origin. In 126 BC a traveller called Chang Ch'ien returned from the country of Ta Yuan; his report is quoted in the *Shih chi*, a large historical compilation of very few years later. The people of Ta Yuan grew grapes as well as wheat and rice; lived in small walled towns; and had 'the offspring of Supernatural Horses'.

Ta Yuan, also called Ferghana, seems to straddle modern Uzbekskaya and Kirgizskaya, on the Jaxartes and not far north of the Pamirs; midway between Sinkiang and the Caspian, it was on the northern of the two routes available to the Chinese travelling to the west. It was an outlying part of ancient Bactria, and had clearly been Hellenised by the Greeks.

On the Chinese side of Ta Yuan lived a nomadic people called the Wu-sun, who also had good horses. In 115 BC, after another journey, Chang Ch'ien brought back several dozen. Like everyone else in that part of the world, the Wu-sun were threatened by the Huns, and therefore anxious for an alliance with the Chinese. This was to be cemented by the marriage of an imperial Chinese princess to the king of the Wu-sun, purchased with a thousand Wu-sun horses.

The horses arrived, and the princess was sent off in 107 BC. She had a miserable life in a tent, about which she wrote a tearful poem. The horses which her misery bought were not, however, as good as the Chinese had expected. In retrospect this is hardly suprising. Since the Wu-sun were still nomads they had not been Hellenised, their horses had probably benefited to an extent by contact with their settled and civilised neighbours to the west, but they were a far cry from the true Nisaeans.

Meanwhile more and more merchants from China visited Ta Yuan, bringing back lucerne and grape-vines; although they brought back a few horses, they were never allowed any of the very best, which were kept locked up in a fortified city called Er-shih. China's northern frontier was now more seriously threatened and deeply penetrated by the mobile Huns, and the Middle Kingdom's need for good horses became acute. The Emperor Wu, a man of energy and vision if not in all respects wise, was determined to get at least a breeding nucleus of the Supernatural Horses of Ta Yuan. He therefore sent a mission, laden with gold coins and a golden statuette of a horse, with which he hoped to buy some of the precious horses of Er-shih. But the people of Ta Yuan were unimpressed. They had grown to dislike and distrust the Chinese merchants who visited them (some of whom had evidently cheated them) and China was too far away to be a useful military ally. They refused both coins and statue. The emperor's ambassadors were so angry that they smashed the golden figure. This insult in turn enraged the people of Ta Yuan, who murdered the ambassadors and took their money.

This atrocity, and still more his undiminished need for good horses, prompted the Emperor Wu to mount, in 104 BC, one of the most disastrous expeditions in military history. The emperor's favourite concubine at the time was a lady called Li. For this reason, which must have seemed adequate at the time, her brother Li Kuang-li was appointed general of an enormous army: 6,000 cavalry (on indifferent horses, of course) and perhaps a third of a million foot soldiers. Li Kuang-li was given the special title of Er-shih General, since the horses of Er-shih were the sole object of the operation.

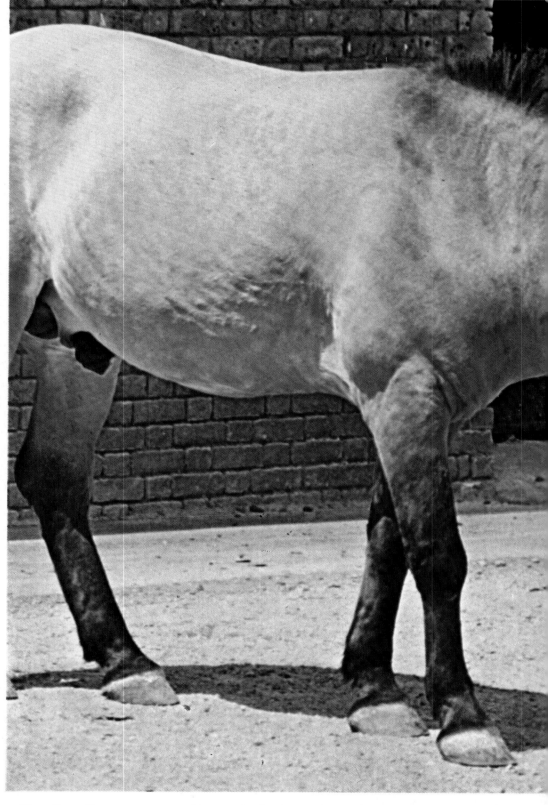

The first disaster was a plague of locusts on the route, which destroyed all foodstuffs for beasts and men. Seeing how the army was weakened, the cities of Sinkiang barred their gates and refused hospitality. When the starving army reached the frontier of Ta Yuan it was routed. Li Kuang-li limped home, two years after setting out, with one tenth of his force and no Supernatural Horses.

But the emperor's need for horses was as pressing as ever, and in 102 BC he mounted another expedition, recruited from the whole of China; the *Shih chi* records a force of 60,000 fighting men, not counting non-combatants, 100,000 oxen, 30,000 horses (still

bad ones), and unnumbered mules, donkeys and camels. Two expert horsemasters were given high official rank and attached to the General Staff. Li Kuang-li was reappointed general, which suggests that his sister's influence over the emperor was still irresistible.

This time there were no locusts. The cities on the route saw a very different army approaching, and meekly provisioned it. One battle had to be fought on the way, and there was some disease and desertion; but half the Chinese army reached the walls of Ershih. They won a battle outside the city, which they settled down to besiege. The people of the city knew exactly what the Chinese wanted, and knew that Mu-kua, King

of Ta Yuan, was refusing to give it to them. After forty days of siege they accordingly cut off Mu-kua's head and sent it to the Chinese. With the head they offered a batch of their horses, in return for the withdrawal of the army. If the Chinese persisted in the war they would, they said, kill all the horses the Chinese had come so far to get.

Li Kuang-li naturally accepted these terms; he took delivery of thirty or forty of the very best 'offspring of Supernatural Horses' and about 3,000 of lower class. When he reached home he had only a fraction of his army left (owing less to military action than to the incompetence and greed of the officers, says the *Shih chi*); but he had

Above: Probably the first kind of horse to be harnessed, if not ridden, by the Chinese: the Prjevalsky. SPECTRUM COLOUR LIBRARY

what mattered to Wu and the empire.

For some time, meanwhile, Wu had been trying to encourage horse-breeding as extensively as possible – the scale of his military problems required immense quantity as well as quality – but without much success. Central China was densely populated, and in many areas short of water: there was enough for harvestable crops but not for forage. The northern provinces, on the line of the Great Wall, were more suitable, and from 112 BC horse breeding was there stimulated by

imperial decree: mares were lent to farmers by the government in return for a stated number of foals.

This is the sort of remount scheme which every government requiring cavalry has undertaken through history, with almost the single exception of the British, who consequently found themselves at the beginning of successive wars desperately short of chargers and troop-horses; at the beginning of the Boer War thousands of indifferent horses had to be bought, from Hungary and elsewhere, at inflated prices, because there was no subsidised and government-sponsored remount scheme of the sort Wu founded.

Horse-breeding in China was never successful on a large scale, however, even in the north. Yet the empire acquired, within two generations, all the horses it needed when the horses bred by the 'offspring of Supernatural Horses' mounted the Chinese cavalry of the northern frontier so well that they were able, for a time, to outride and outfight the Huns. The latters' Mongolian ponies were entirely adequate for most purposes, but they were no match for the descendants of the Nisaeans in a cavalry action. Wu's victories over the Huns brought periods of peace, during which there was extensive trade between the Huns and the Chinese. The Huns got silk and gold, the Chinese got horses.

The supply of horses to China depended not on Chinese breeding but on importation that followed peace, which followed military victory; this hinged on quite small forces of very well-mounted cavalry; this relied on the securing of superior horses from the far west, which hinged on the huge expeditions commanded by Li Kuang-li against Ta Yuan.

The expeditions of 104 and 102 BC had the effect of pacifying the trade-route to the west, establishing Chinese military prestige along the route, and opening up a far higher volume of trade and travel. Historians of art and philosophy remark on the transformation of Chinese civilisation by the importation, along this route, of designs and forms and ideas. Most important of the last, perhaps, was Buddhism, which is said to have arrived in China from India in 2 BC.

Not only, therefore, did a handful of good horses save the Chinese Empire from the Huns: but also the titanic effort required to get the horses – an effort that had no other object – resulted in the transformation of the Empire and of its art and religion. Since the general who made it all possible owed his appointment to his sister's charms, the sex-appeal of the Lady Li had a greater influence on the course of civilisation than that of any other concubine in history.

The War Horses of Genghis Khan

Genghis Khan, one of the great conquerors in the history of the world, was born in the year AD 1162. His father, Yesukai, was a powerful Mongol overlord who ruled a vast barren region to the west of the Great Wall of China. On the death of his father the young Genghis Khan – still known as Temujin, the name that he retained for another thirty years – was involved for three years in tribal wars against those who refused to show him allegiance. Lacking support, he was compelled to retire to Karakhoum (Karakorum), capital city of Toghrul Khan whose daughter he married. Toghrul appointed him commander of his army, but Genghis proved so successful a general that his father-in-law and his courtiers, jealous of his growing reputation, attempted to assassinate him. He fled, but later returned at the head of an army 5,000 strong, routed Toghrul and seized his dominions. Within a year Genghis Khan was ruler of all Mongolia.

His brilliance as a leader was confirmed to the tribesmen in AD 1206 when a priest announced that it had been ordained that Genghis Khan should govern the entire earth. Five years later he prepared to attack China, raised an army which included 30,000 cavalry, and crossed the Great Wall. After three years of fierce fighting Peking was captured by his Mongol hordes and the Emperor fled. Genghis Khan became the supreme master of the entire North Chinese territory from Mongolia to Korea. He next turned his attention to the west claiming, 'there cannot be two suns in the heaven, nor two Kha-Khans upon the earth'. Determined to vanquish his supposed enemies he invaded Persia, Afghanistan and the lands to the north of these countries. In the first year of a campaign which was to last for seven years he captured Bokhara and Samarkand, before ordering his hordes to march further westwards to the shores of the Caspian sea. His armies subjugated the Caucasus and, penetrating deeper into Russia, plundered the land between the Volga and the Dnieper before returning to Mongolia.

The administration of his vast empire stretched his resources to the limit. He built roads and at twenty-five mile intervals erected station forts. Almost ten thousand of these forts were established, from where teams of dispatch riders could gallop their hardy ponies over the rugged mountainous roads delivering messages and news of war. Most of these ponies, small and sturdy with coarse heads and thick necks, were bred in the plains to the north of the Gobi desert. The Mongol warriors captured them by the primitive method of lassoing them around the neck, and following them on horseback until their

Above: Genghis Khan praying in the Kipchak Steppe during the campaign in China. BRITISH MUSEUM, LONDON

Left: Genghis Khan fighting the Chinese in the mountains.
BRITISH MUSEUM, LONDON

Overleaf: The coffin of Genghis Khan borne by his warriors.
BRITISH MUSEUM, LONDON

captive became exhausted. Although merciless in time of war, the Mongolians treated their horses with care and devotion. When a great Mongolian horse died his owner pulled some of the hairs from his mane and tail and used them as strings on a musical instrument with which he would travel far, singing songs of praise about his horse.

Despite the fact that Genghis Khan was reputed to have massacred five million people at the hands of his barbaric followers who showed no mercy to their defeated enemies, he was considered a great administrator. He exempted priests and physicians from taxes and military service, and created severe laws against theft. Exhausted by years of toil and conquest he died in 1227 after being thrown from his horse whilst hunting the wild horses of Arbukha. One of his last acts before he died was to order the execution of a defeated chieftain.

The Battle of Hastings

In the autumn of 1066 William of Normandy waited patiently for a favourable wind to bring his invasion fleet across the Channel, and an English army commanded by their King, Harold, watched for his arrival from the clifftops of southern England. During the weeks of frustrating inactivity the harvest made urgent claims on Harold's soldiers and it became impossible for him to maintain supplies and discipline. Much of his army had dispersed when the news came that the north had been invaded and he was compelled to march to York where he defeated the King of Norway at Stamford Bridge. Meanwhile, the south wind had strengthened in the Channel and William hastily embarked his troops, knights and cavalry, and landed unopposed at Pevensey Bay on 29 September.

The Battle of Hastings has been described as 'a victory over infantry by cavalry supported by the long-range weapon of the archers', for William had both cavalry and archers, whilst Harold fought behind the shield of his closely packed infantry.

Harold had been forced by William's initiative to fight a defensive battle, but was able to take his stand in a superb natural position at the top of Senlac ridge which was flanked by steep slopes running down to marshy ground on both sides. For much of 14 October the English held their ground as the knights of Normandy, France, Flanders and Brittany continually charged their solid ranks. The knights did not have enough weight to break through the English line, and their horses, which were not armoured, refused to face the javelins, axes and stones hurled down the slopes by the defenders. Most of the charges ended in fierce hand-to-hand fighting, with no obvious advantage to either side.

The dispirited Normans could not smash Harold's unyielding army, and might never have done so but for a tactical error on the part of the English. As the Norman cavalry turned back from one of their unsuccessful assaults and started trotting down the slope in disarray, some of the more impetuous English, contrary to Harold's orders, followed, only to be slaughtered by mounted knights. As the day progressed the Normans were ordered by William, mounted on a war-horse given to him by the King of Spain, to feign similar retreats. Gradually, the English army was destroyed.

By nightfall the battle was over, won by the cunning use of the invading cavalry. Harold was dead – although historians do not agree that he was shot through the eye by an arrow – and the road to London was open to William.

From the Bayeux Tapestry:
Below: The Norman army goes into battle.
Above, right: The English resist the Norman attack.
Below, right: Men and horses killed.
Following spread: Norman knights attack.
ALL: MICHAEL HOLFORD LIBRARY

Agincourt

The defeat of Charles VI's army by Henry V at Agincourt was described by one French chronicler as 'the most disgraceful event that had ever happened to the Kingdom of France'.

Sixty-seven years before Henry's coronation in 1413 his great-grandfather, Edward III, had won his great victory over the French at Crecy and ten years later Henry's grandfather, the Black Prince, had again defeated them at Poitiers.

Edward III had gained absolute control of great territories in France but thereafter a steady decline had set in and, on succeeding to the throne, Henry V was determined to do something about this decline. His French rival, Charles VI, was only forty-four at the time but was plagued by a wife who detested him. Prematurely old, he was occasionally stricken with mad fits and his country, at the beginning of the century the most prosperous power in Europe, was being

torn apart by rivalries, resentments and jealousies. It was therefore a propitious time for Henry V to revive the claims of his ancestors and by 1414 he was actively preparing for war. He had plenty of support, for those who were to fight in France relished the prospect in which they could see much profit and adventure. But, more important for the upper classes, France for a long time had been a military training ground which was infinitely more thrilling than the forays

endured in Wales and Scotland and had given England's war-leaders a taste for campaigning and a desire for more profitable and exciting action.

The true knights of the day looked favourably on a full-scale war where they could transfer their tournaments from the lists to the battlefield and indulge their passion for aggressive tests of skill and virility against opponents they regarded with a mixture of reluctant admiration, envy and frustration.

Logistical problems for mounting an expedition to the Continent were immense even in those days and transport for the horses was a particularly important consideration. A duke was allowed fifty horses for his own use, an earl twenty-four, a knight six, an esquire four and a horse archer one. Specialist troops also took horses with them and together with hundreds of pack animals as many as 25,000 horses sailed with the 1415 expedition.

These figures are interesting and emphasise the trends that had developed. Edward I's army on the Continent in 1297 had mustered only some 900 cavalry compared with 8,000 infantry. Edward III's army contained a higher proportion of cavalry, the additional mounted men being horse archers who could pursue the retreating enemy at great speed after his cavalry attack had been stopped and broken by the line of armoured knights and foot archers.

At three o'clock on Sunday afternoon, 11 August 1415, with drums beating on deck and trumpeters blowing their horns, sailors shouting and priests praying, Henry's great armada weighed anchor and sailed for France.

Three days later the invasion had begun and Harfleur was quickly and successfully put to siege. But Henry's forces had been badly reduced through the garrison he had to leave there, the casualties suffered and the sickness which had overtaken his men. Now with only 6,000 men, of which 1,000 were men-at-arms and 5,000 archers, the risks of continuing his advance were clear. He decided to continue, however, and set off north along the road to Calais that was to lead to the Battle of Agincourt.

On 24 October 1415 his flank guards reported that many thousands of the enemy were drawing close to him and Henry knew that the battle he had provoked was upon him. The next day his army went forward to within 300 yards of the French and let fly their piercing arrows. Attacked, the French army sprang to life. Their mounted men-at-arms on the flanks, or as many of them as could push through to the front, charged; for the French still believed in the medieval cliché that 'a hundred horses are worth a thousand foot'.

Those who galloped forward found their horses impaled on the sharp points of the fences of stakes with which the English had surrounded themselves. Horses wounded by arrow heads that tore deep gashes in their flesh ran away in all directions but mainly towards their own lines, knocking down the knights who, burdened by the weight of their armour, were unable to get up again out of the wet and glutinous earth.

Contemptuous of the events shaping before their eyes the French refused to accept the socially inferior archer as a worthy opponent for a knight in armour and continued their approach on the English line with their traditional pride and bravery, but their men-at-arms were so thickly packed in rigid formation that there was no room for them to fight. The English continued to cut the French down in their hundreds throwing themselves upon their enemy in a fury that soon had the dead and wounded lying in heaps where many of the wounded died from suffocation.

Soon after mid-day no Frenchman was left on the field and, though unscathed, the third line viewing the scene from a distance showed no stomach for the fight. Even now, the French outnumbered the English but they were disorganised and no leaders emerged, men refusing to serve under banners other than their own and knights refusing to accept orders from other knights.

But the French prisoners who had been taken as part of the booty of warfare had become a problem and Henry decided he could no longer spare the men or resources required to look after them and, fearing another French attack, to the dismay of his troops ordered that they should be killed. Fortunately this wholesale massacre was halted when it became clear that the French were not capable of counter-attack.

After a battle which had lasted for about three hours the total number of French dead was believed to be about 9,000 with 1,500 French noblemen taken prisoner. Henry had acquitted himself well, the English casualties totalling a mere 500!

When he had landed in France, King Henry V knelt in prayer. On returning home he again prayed on the beach at Dover and at Canterbury at the shrine of St Thomas, kissing the saint's holy relics. God had brought him victory and, with His help, Henry was determined to make himself worthy of it.

Knights in Armour

In England the word knight is derived from the Saxon *kneht*, meaning a man-at-arms or servant to the king, and originally had little association with horses. On the Continent, however, the words *chevalier*, *cavalliere* and *caballero* prove the close link between Frenchmen, Italians and Spaniards and their horses.

The institution of knighthood gradually evolved throughout Europe and in Britain was first advanced by King Arthur and his Knights of the Round Table.

In Saxon times knighthood was conferred by the priest after solemn confession and a midnight church vigil. The new knight would offer his sword on the altar to acknowledge his devotion to the church and his avowed intention to lead a holy life. He would then give the church a sum of money to redeem his sword, which the priest would gird upon him, after striking him a blow on the cheek or shoulder – implying that this was the last affront that he should ever endure without retaliating. He then took an oath to protect the distressed and to maintain right against might. If he ever

failed to honour his oath his sword might be broken, his escutcheon reversed and his spurs smashed . . .

The medieval knight in armour did not become a fighting force with which to be reckoned until the introduction of stirrups. Although some of the Asiatics who invaded Europe in AD 100 had used stirrups it was not until the era of Charlemagne (AD 742–814) that they were adopted by western civilisation. Their adoption was revolutionary, for it enabled a heavily armoured horseman to retain his balance in the saddle whilst using a weighty spear, sword or lance. Previously a chevalier so armed, and wearing mail shirt and helmet weighing some 40 lb would have fallen from his

horse if he had attempted any aggressive action against his enemy.

The shirt of mail, known on the Continent as a hauberk, was a garment made of small steel rings which were interwoven, and reached to the wearer's knees. Usually the knight wore clothes made of soft leather under his mail. This type of armour offered little protection against experienced and accurate longbowmen, and fell into disuse in the fourteenth century, being replaced by heavier plate armour. Kings and emperors wore elaborate and complicated suits of armour often engraved and inlaid with gold. Knights began to wear breastplates, leg harness, armoured gauntlets and helmets with visors. It

became the custom for them to wear above their armour a loose-fitting blouse on which were emblazoned their arms, thus originating the expression 'coat of arms'.

In times of peace the knights enjoyed jousting at tournaments where they could exhibit their courage, chivalry and prowess with their weapons. The earliest tournaments were held in France, where they were probably instituted by the ancestors of the Counts of Anjou. In England many such tournaments and pageants were held in the tiltyard in the part of London that is now Smithfield Market. In France the death of King Henry II in 1559 as a result of the loss of an eye whilst participating in a tourna-

ment led to the abandonment of the pastime.

In times of war the knight went to battle with his armourer, his prized warhorses and his lesser valued coursers. Shakespeare's *Henry V* contains the lines:

Steed threatens steed, in high and
    boastful neighs
Piercing the night's dull ear, and from
    the tents
The armourers, accomplishing the
    knights
With busy hammers, closing rivets up,
Give dreadful note of preparation.

The end of the use of knights as an

Left: A 13th-century bronze aquamanile in the shape of a knight on horseback.
BRITISH MUSEUM, LONDON

Above: Two jousting knights from a 15th-century English heraldic manuscript.
BRITISH MUSEUM, LONDON

Overleaf: Medieval knights and their standards.

effective arm of war came with the greater power of artillery in the middle of the sixteenth century. The range and power of cannons and guns put paid to their role as battle-winning cavalry, but failed to destroy their romantic reputation for chivalry which has lasted until the present day.

Herzog Cristof von Payrn

Herzog Fridrich von Sachssen

The Battle of the Spurs

Four years after his ascent to the throne, Henry VJII found his plans ripe for the invasion of France. Long years of peace contributed to make the project popular and on 30 June 1513 Henry, with a vanguard of 8,000 men leavened with a body of English archers, landed at Calais. Despite the growing use of fire-arms these archers were still renowned throughout Europe.

Henry, though fired with the spirit of martial enterprise, was shrewd enough to advance 120,000 crowns to the Emperor Maximilian, thus ensuring his support. Armed with pike and sword, the Swiss, also regarded as allies, kept their word and supported the King. Maximilian, however, could not raise the complement of auxiliaries required but was chivalrous enough to enlist himself in the King of England's service. Henry, touched with his magnanimous gesture, appointed the

Left: Henry VIII with Knights Companion
of the Garter.
BRITISH MUSEUM, LONDON. PHOTOGRAPH,
J. R. FREEMAN AND CO

Overleaf: An unknown artists' depiction of
the Battle of the Spurs.
BY GRACIOUS PERMISSION OF HER MAJESTY
THE QUEEN

Emperor to direct the combined operations.

The small town of Teronane was first successfully besieged but the French King, Louis, with some cunning, advancing to Amiens despatched a body of 800 light horse under Fontrailles to create a diversion. This body was successful enough and surprised the English camp but lacked the strength to maintain their advantage. Meanwhile, anticipating the main advance of the French cavalry, Henry ordered a body of English troops to cross the Lis in readiness.

Suddenly confronted with this unexpected opposition the French fell into one of the most unaccountable panics in military history – a lapse all the more remarkable because the force consisted of the Gentlemen of France. A mad *Sauve qui peut!* ensued and in the headlong flight which ensued the flower of French chivalry and cavalry was mercilessly cut down or captured. Chevalier Bayard, a knight *Sans peur et sans reproche*, was among the prisoners captured, together with the Duc de Longueville, the General in Command.

This amazing incident left a straight, clear road to Paris but, as was later manifestly clear, Henry had designed this expedition for glory not for conquest!

The Bataile of
Spvrrs anno
1513

The Battle of Marston Moor

The Civil War of 1642-46 has been described as the most decisive event in English history, for the failure of the Royalist armies who supported the cause of King Charles I to withstand their antagonists resulted in the triumph of the Parliamentary institutions. *If* is a dubious word at any time, but *if* the anti-monarchists had lost the day then it is probable that they would have emigrated in their thousands to America. Enterprising merchants, skilled craftsmen and men from every walk of life who believed in Liberty would have crossed the Atlantic to New England, and it is unlikely that a revolt would have ever again been contemplated against a Royal Church and a Royal State.

At Nottingham on 22 August 1642 the Royal Standard was raised to be greeted by 'God save King Charles and hang up the Roundheads'. Two months later the rival armies of the King and the Parliamentarians fought a drawn battle at Edgehill. For the next twenty months inconclusive campaigns were carried out in various parts of the kingdom whilst Cromwell steadily increased the efficiency of the New Model Army and the followers of the King appeared to hold north Yorkshire and the lands to the Scottish border. However, the Battle of Marston Moor destroyed the hopes of the Royalists in the north of England and proved to be one of the decisive battles in the Civil War.

Although the Parliamentary forces, comprising three armies from East Anglia, Scotland and the north of England, heavily outnumbered their opponents, especially in the infantry, the Royalists came so near to winning that the elderly Earl of Leven, the senior general on the Parliamentary side, was absent when the battle was won. He had fled precipitately to Leeds, thinking all was lost, and had to return shamefacedly to the scene of the battle after he had heard of the Parliamentary victory.

Twenty-three-year-old Prince Rupert and his cavalry had skilfully deceived the Parliamentary forces, evaded their waiting army which was blocking the Knaresborough-to-York road at Marston, eight miles to the west of the city, and raised the siege of York behind their backs. The following morning, 2 July, Rupert arrived on Marston Moor eager to attack at once while the enemy were uncertain of his intentions and unprepared for battle. Unfortunately, he was compelled to wait until late afternoon before the Earl of Newcastle, whom he had antagonised, brought his infantry from York. By then the chance of surprise had vanished.

Towards dusk Prince Rupert retired to eat a frugal supper, having given up

all hope of joining battle. At that moment Cromwell decided to charge. In Rupert's absence his subordinate cavalry commander on the Royalist right wing, Lord Byron, soon ran into difficulties against the best troops in the Parliamentary army, Cromwell's cavalry from the Eastern Association. On the other flank, however, the position was reversed, and Lord Goring's Royalist cavalry were so much in the ascendant that the infantry in the centre of the Parliamentary line became exposed to cavalry attack, and many of the Scots

infantry fled from the battle.

Prince Rupert, roused to action, came successfully to Byron's aid and the issue hung in the balance in the cavalry battle which followed on that flank. At this vital moment, with Cromwell slightly wounded in the neck and temporarily out of action, the Scot Leslie brought up his reserve of cavalry. Although his men numbered only two thousand and rode 'little light Scottish nags', they took Rupert's cavalry in the flank when the Prince's troops were already heavily engaged with Cromwell's men. Their

intervention was decisive. Rupert's wing of the Royalist army was routed and fled from the Moor in disarray.

The disciplined cavalry of the Eastern Association were then seen at their best. Instead of dashing from the battle after their fleeing enemy in the fashion of Rupert at Edgehill, they halted, reformed and under the control of Cromwell wheeled right before trotting round behind the main Royalist lines whence they charged the rear of the victorious left wing of the Royalists under Goring. It was the turning point

Above: Cromwell at the Battle of Marston Moor leading a charge after being wounded in the arm. MARY EVANS PICTURE LIBRARY

Overleaf: Cromwell after the Battle of Marston Moor, by Ernest Croft. BURNLEY ART GALLERY

of the battle, broke the Royalist resistance and brought success to the Parliamentarians. By midnight the final shot had been fired and the final surrender made in the bloodiest battle of the Civil War.

Gustavus Adolphus

With the development of the long pike and the increased use of powder and shot in battle the picturesque pageantry of the battlefield and the role of horse and the cavalry underwent a great change. No one was more responsible than Gustavus Adolphus, King of Sweden from 1594 to 1632. An innovator and military architect of great flair, Gustavus with short, light brown hair and brownish yellow beard was nicknamed 'The Lion of the North' and possessed an inventiveness and organising genius which has assured his place in military history. Dressing simply himself, in an unadorned coat of buff cloth, leather riding breeches and long boots, he lightened the load of his cavalrymen, banished the slow, ponderous methods of fighting with pistols which had been adopted by cavalrymen of that era and went back to shock action with the sword, using firearms only when speed and mobility were not needed. If the basis of all modern tactics is a team of combined arms then Gustavus was the true originator, his objective always being to have the three principal arms – infantry, artillery and cavalry – working in support of each other.

Gustavus had also managed to enrol into his forces six regiments of Scottish soldiers under the command of the Duke of Hamilton. These Scots were past masters in the art of fighting on horseback and both soldiers and their mounts were well disciplined. These qualities coupled with Gustavus's superb knowledge of cavalry tactics and great imaginative flair became a formidable combination.

In his early campaigns in Livonia the Polish cavalry had greatly impressed Gustavus. The hard-riding Polish lancers and swordsmen, relying on shock, rather than fire-power, had continually tested his own cumbersome mounted pistoleers. This decided Gustavus to reorganise his cavalry and he formed them into cuirassiers and dragoon regiments, each comprising eight companies or squadrons of 152 horsemen. Armed with a sword and two pistols these cuirassiers charged at full gallop and relied mostly on the sword. For their part, the dragoons were armed with a musket and sabre and an axe for general use in making or destroying obstacles. Gustavus placed great faith in his cavalry and, for the sake of manoeuvrability in combat, put his horsemen in line rather than in column, each line being three ranks deep.

Inheriting three unfinished wars with Denmark, Poland and Russia he decided that the conflict with Denmark was the most dangerous and urgent, and that Russia and Poland could be left until later. He settled the conflict with Denmark and by 1617 had forced Russia to agree to his tough demands.

For the next thirteen years he busied himself with campaigns which were designed to establish the complete dominance of Sweden over the shores of the Baltic and veritably turn it into a Swedish lake. By 1632 he had become the most powerful man in Europe, dominating northern, central and western Germany.

The decisive battle of his career took place on the Plain of Lutzen when he decided to eliminate the crafty, barbaric Czecho-Slovakian General Wallenstein whose manner of war was to shed little blood and to avoid a battle if he could do so without imperilling the cause he served. The Imperial Forces against Gustavus were more numerous than his own and occupied a more advantageous position. Gustavus, wishing to attack before Pappenheim reinforced Wallenstein's army and believing in the principle that it was well to wash oneself completely when in the bath and 'in war it is the favourable moment which decides everything', decided to attack.

In the disposition of his forces the wings were made up mainly of cavalry in two lines and his reserve contained six squadrons of cavalry. His army spent the night in battle order, the troops a mile from the enemy sleeping in their starting positions. The flames from the burning Lutzen and the camp fires were plainly visible to the opposing armies. The Swedish drums roused Gustavus's soldiers in the early dawn, prayers were said and hymns sung in each regiment and squadron as the men fell in and Gustavus, wearing a swordproof shirt of elkhide under his coat, galloped from unit to unit amidst great cheering.

Early in the battle his troops suffered a set back and to relieve the pressure on his centre he pulled one of his cavalry regiments out of the line and led it at a gallop towards the threatened centre. As in all battles, confusion reigned but riding ahead with his escort, as was his practice, Gustavus became isolated and unexpectedly ran into a detachment of Imperial Cuirassiers who opened fire and killed him; his riderless horse covered with blood, galloping back to the Swedish lines, announced his death. Enraged rather than dispirited by this terrible news his troops went on to a great victory. Gustavus was only thirty-eight when he perished and his death was mourned throughout most of Europe, it even being alleged that the Emperor Ferdinand shed crocodile tears at the news!

Right: Gustavus Adolphus, 'Christian King of Sweden', with his aid and champion Johann Georgen Hertzogen zu Gachsen. BRITISH MUSEUM, LONDON

Waare Abbildung
Ihrer Königlichen Mayestät / Herrn GVSTAV ADOLPHI, Christlichen Königs in Schweden/ꝛc.
Vnd
Ihrer Chur Fürstlichen Durchleuchtigkeit/Herrn Johann
Georgen Hertzogen zu Sachsen/vnd Chur Fürsten/ꝛc.

Gott   mit   Vns

Wie wunderbarlich das Glück sey/
Daß haben wir erfahren frey/
Anfangs die gfahr nit war gering/
Da der Feind zufechten anfieng/
Denn Er war starck vnd vnverzagt/
Sein beste Schantz hat Er gewagt/
Vns Königs Cron/zween Churröck es galt/

Allein war Gott mit vns im Streit/
Ihm sey Lob/Ehr/vnd Preiß allzeit/
Derhat es gnädig so gewendt/
Daß der Sieg kam in vnsre Händt/
Darob wir in Gott frölich sein/
Vnd geben Ihm die Ehr allein/
Vnd bitten Ihn/daß mehr Sieg vnd Heil

Sobieski - King John III

Young as he was when he died at Lutzen, the fame of Gustavus Adolphus lived on, and his successful tactics of feint and assault were to be copied and employed by all the great horsemen of the seventeenth century. One of these was John Sobieski who was once a horseman bodyguard in the service of Louis XIV of France.

Sobieski had fought against the Cossacks, the Tartars and the Russians. Against these great horsemen, probably the best in the world at that time, he had been an eye-witness of the full capa-

bilities of cavalry and the war-horse, and harnessing this knowledge to imaginative tactics brought him the victories in battle which made him famous.

In 1667 he routed 100,000 Tartars with an army of only 20,000 by a clever flanking cavalry manoeuvre. His next victim was the Pasha of Damascus who was leading an army of some 200,000 against Sobieski's 10,000 horsemen! Probably his greatest victory was achieved in 1683, when he drove the Turkish army of Kara Mustapha across Hungary, the savagery of his pursuit

routing a bewildered enemy who had never before seen such tactics employed against them.

John Sobieski had been well schooled in Louis XIV's stables, where he learned the then little-known skills of breeding from Arabic strains with as much emphasis on endurance as on speed. He was a great and discerning horseman and was under no illusion of the power which efficient cavalry bestowed upon any nation who harnessed it.

When he was made King of Poland he was prepared to prove his faith by spend-ing great amounts of his own money. He set up good stables, splendidly equipped horse-training schools, and led the way in breeding fine horses at stud. This expertise soon spread throughout Europe and later in the eighteenth century led to both horses and riders being trained in the Haute Ecole which, despite so much unpopularity with the English, did prove effective in battle, by co-ordinating both the horse's strength and beauty so that he would respond to the lightest hand of any rider.

The feats of Sobieski's charger *Palasz*

Above: John III and the liberation of Vienna, AD 1683.
BRITISH MUSEUM, LONDON

(Sabre) emblazons Polish history. This horse, a big weight-carrying grey stallion and a cross between Andalusian, Oriental and native breeds, carried Sobieski throughout his campaigns against invading Turks and Cossacks and led the charge that shattered the Turks at Vienna and the battle that earned his master the soubriquet 'The Saviour of Vienna'.

The Battle of Blenheim

The Duke of Marlborough's original plan was to capture Blenheim village and then 'roll up' the French line from the south. But on meeting fierce resistance he decided to fight a containing action both there and in the north where Prince Eugene met equally tough opposition from the troops under Maréchal Marsin. So successful were these containing actions that Blenheim became heavily overcrowded with French troops, who had been rushed in to meet the English attacks, and the wide French centre was left dangerously weak.

Consequently, Marlborough was able to launch his major attack in the centre, and to use his cavalry with great success. The Nebel was not a large stream, but it was difficult to cross in places, particularly for the cavalry and artillery. Yet, facing Marlborough, Maréchal Tallard preferred to ignore his advantage, allowing the enemy to cross unhindered except by artillery fire, in the belief that he could soon drive them back in confusion and trap them in the swampy ground beside the stream.

As a result of these various events Marlborough achieved that significant superiority of numbers at the vital place and at the crucial hour of the battle, late in the afternoon. Once he had survived a fierce attack from the direction of Oberglau which was spearheaded by the 'wild geese' or Irish troops serving with the French, Marlborough swept all before him in the centre. He launched a combined cavalry and infantry attack which soon overwhelmed the young French infantry, who fought bravely although deserted by their own cavalry, and then was able to wheel left and encircle Blenheim from the rear.

Marsin, seeing the right half of the French line crumble, prudently withdrew his troops in good order, but Tallard and those under his command were not so successful. Tallard himself was forced to surrender and was allowed to observe the final defeat of his army from the safety of Marlborough's own coach, but many of his troops were less fortunate. Thousands of French cavalry dashed headlong from the battlefield, hoping to escape across the Danube.

The fortunes of those in Blenheim were no better. Their commander, Clérambault, deserted and plunged into the Danube on his horse, never emerging to explain his behaviour. Eventually the large number of French who had been crammed into the village were persuaded to surrender, although much against the wishes of the majority.

The overwhelming victory is not now considered as primarily a triumph for Marlborough's cavalry as it once was. His cavalry had merely applied the *coup de grâce*, and Tallard's cavalry by comparison had provided only feeble resistance; although it must be remembered that this was partly due to disease that had been widespread among their horses for some weeks before the battle.

THE GLORIOUS BATTLE
of BLENHEIM.

Above: The Battle of Blenheim.
MARY EVANS PICTURE LIBRARY

**The Battle of Blenheim depicted in the
Blenheim Tapestry, Blenheim Palace.**
HIS GRACE THE DUKE OF MARLBOROUGH

47

Frederich Wilhelm von Seydlitz

It was at the Battle of Mollwitz in 1741 that Frederick the Great learned the quality of cavalry. The Austrian cavalry in a sudden charge shattered the Prussians and Frederick with his defeated cavalry around him was forced to flee from his first battle. His forces had no answer to the Austrian horsemen's tactics of a heavy charge, with pistols fired from the saddle, followed by razor-sharp sabre strokes at the heads of their opponent's horses and finally, as they hurtled past, a backward slash which cut down the riders. Frederick fled from the battlefield and never again alluded to it. He had learned his lesson well, however, and began the systematic retraining of the Prussian cavalry. Later at the Battle of Rossbach in 1757 the proof of his thoroughness and method was exemplified by one of the most rapid victories of all his campaigns.

The officer who engineered this was Frederich Wilhelm von Seydlitz, later to become known as the Prince of Dragoons and one of the most famous cavalry commanders of his age.

At this time he was thirty-six years of age and had served with all branches of the cavalry. He first came to the notice of Frederick at the disastrous Battle of Kolin in 1757 and was rapidly promoted to lieutenant-general. No one questioned his advancement. He was chivalrous, fair and just and was blessed with a flair which allowed him quickly to sum up a situation and strike at the right moment.

A master tactician in the field, he was a great trainer of horses and horsemen and moulded in the tradition of men who school horses and become involved in the minutia of horse care and husbandry. His swordsmanship was legendary and it is said that he frequently displayed this to his troops in a 'show off' exhibition of splitting with his sabre an apple thrown into the air by one of his men while he was at full gallop.

His golden opportunity to make history occurred at Rossbach on 5 November 1757. His forces were outnumbered two to one by an allied army from French and German states. The handling of his small force by von

Seydlitz was superb, every crisis in the battle being resolved by his genius. It was inevitable, however, that his brilliance should attract clashes, and these followed at the Battle of Zorndorf in 1758 and at Kunersdorf in 1759.

At Zorndorf the King ordered him to advance with his cavalry upon the Russian gun-emplacements. He twice refused his Sovereign's orders and, at the third command, Frederick informed him that he would answer for such disobedience with his head. Von Seydlitz, as imperturbable as ever, replied, 'Sire, after the battle, my head will be at the service of the King,' whereupon he executed two masterly pincer movements upon the enemy which ensured victory and the King's pardon and embrace.

At Kunersdorf, the King, unwisely did not heed his brilliant young commander's advice. Ordered to advance by the King, von Seydlitz's instinct warned him against it. The King, however, was adamant and advancing against the Russian might von Seydlitz was wounded and his squadrons of horse suffered severely. Frederick, beside himself with rage, was carried from the field by his own hussars. In the event, his enemy did not follow up their advantage but there is no doubt that had he heeded the great cavalry commander's advice a sweeter victory might have been achieved.

Facing page: Frederick the Great at the Battle of Leutzen.
BRITISH MUSEUM, LONDON, PHOTOGRAPH JOHN R. FREEMAN AND CO

Below: Frederick congratulates General von Seydlitz after the Battle of Zorndorf, 25 August 1758; a painting by R. Knötel, 1895.
BILDARCHIV PREUSSISCHER KULTURBESITZ

The Battle of Dettingen

The war of the Austrian Succession began in 1741. King George II was anxious to support the Austrian interests, but for more than a year his chief minister, Sir Robert Walpole, dissuaded him from such a course of action. Early in 1742 Walpole resigned, to the undisguised delight of the King, and was succeeded by John Carteret who willingly concurred with the King's wish to join forces with Austria and Holland against France.

King George II, a dapper little man with blue eyes and florid complexion, loved the life of a soldier, and to the consternation of his ministers insisted on participating in the ensuing campaign. As a young man he had served under the famous Duke of Marlborough and had been present at the Battle of Oudenarde. He never forgot the thrill and the excitement of the occasion, and longed once again to savour the dangers and the glories of battle. Remembering these experiences he decided that his twenty-one-year-old son William, Duke of Cumberland, should join him on the Continent. There was an ulterior motive for this decision, for the King secretly hoped that the young Duke would gain battle honours and thus strengthen his reputation as a gallant and dashing soldier. Such a reputation might be greatly to his advantage should the question ever arise of disinheriting his elder brother, the Prince of Wales.

The late spring of 1743 was spent by the King and the Duke in Hanover, a small provincial town overshadowed by the magnificence of the Palace of Herrenhausen which lay two miles away. Here the King dallied whilst mock battles, military parades and army manoeuvres were held in his honour. In June, the sixty-one-year-old King and his son joined the allied forces, some 40,000 strong, on the right bank of the River Main. George's personal baggage was gigantic and included more than six hundred horses, eighty wagons and carts and a vast supply of fine wine, damask napkins and bed-linen. The army of which he took command, consisting of a gathering of British, Dutch, Hessians, Hanoverians and Austrians, had originally been formed in the Low Countries before moving slowly into Germany under the generalship of the elderly Lord Stair whose military knowledge had been acquired when he had been one of Marlborough's officers. For a week after his arrival King George II happily inspected his troops, appeared in the best of spirits, and oblivious to the tactical moves being made by the 60,000 French troops under the competent leadership of Marshall Duc de Noailles, who had secured the bridgeheads both above and below the allied army and was threatening to surround them.

Eventually it became apparent that the allies would be compelled to retreat towards Hanau or starve. Realising the inevitable decision which would be made, Noailles had posted his second-in-command, Count Grammont, in a strong position near the village of Dettingen. It seemed that the French held every ace in the pack and that the allies faced either the ignominy of surrender or near annihilation. Their plight was parlous until Grammont, against the orders of Noailles, rashly decided to leave his virtually impregnable position and lead his 28,000 troops in a direct attack on the allied army. Such tactics were sheer folly, and saved the allies.

The King loved every minute of the battle, fought on 27 June, and acquitted himself with great bravery. Flushed with excitement, he sent his aides hither and thither with orders and instructions, flourished his sword and encouraged his soldiers with compliments and praise. At one moment his horse took fright and tried to bolt, but the king, a fine horseman, swiftly brought him under control. Deciding, however, that he could trust his own feet more than those of his horse, he dismounted. Later he advanced towards the French at the head of his troops, shouting in his guttural Germanic accent, 'Now for the honour of England. Fire and behave bravely, and the French will soon run.' The French did not relish the ensuing hand-to-hand combat, had little appetite for the struggle, and began to flee. Many of them were drowned in the river.

Meanwhile, the Duke of Cumberland, behaving courageously on the left wing of the allied forces, kept a cool head when facing a hail of bullets and gained the admiration of his soldiers by his calmness. Shot in the calf of the leg he made little fuss about his injury and impressed a junior officer in the 12th Regiment of Foot who wrote to his father telling him of the Duke's bravery. Years later the officer, as General Wolfe, was to gain immortality on the Heights of Abraham, in the defeat of Montcalm.

The day was also notable for the last creation on the field of battle of a knight banneret. Trooper Thomas Brown of the 3rd Dragoons saw two standards of his regiment cut to atoms and the third drop from the hands of a wounded cornet. As he was retrieving it, a French sabre slashed two fingers from his bridle hand. Uncontrolled, Brown's horse bolted with his rider through the French lines. When at last the charger halted Brown turned, to see coming towards him the very standard he had hoped to save being carried triumphantly by a French cavalryman. Brown slew the carrier, recaptured his standard and single-handed fought his way back through the hostile horse and

foot to his own lines. The king knighted him on the field.

In reality, the battle of Dettingen was an indecisive action and had little effect upon the war. Nevertheless it was acclaimed in England as a glorious victory. When King George II and his son arrived at Gravesend in November they were greeted as heroic and gallant conquerors and were feted on their triumphant journey to St James's Palace. The historical significance of Dettingen

Above: King George II at the Battle of Dettingen, 16 June 1743. The king was the last British sovereign to command a force in the field. Painting by John Wootton.
NATIONAL ARMY MUSEUM, LONDON

was that it was the final occasion upon which an English Sovereign led his troops into battle. It enhanced the reputation and popularity of King George II, and remained for the rest of his life his happiest and most unforgettable memory.

Paul Revere's Ride

Longfellow's famous poem about Paul Revere's ride vividly describes the event on 18 April 1775 which led directly to the fighting at Lexington and Concord between English troops and American rebels, and to the outbreak of the American War of Independence.

A hurry of hoofs in a village street
A shape in the moonlight, a bulk in
  the dark,
And beneath from the pebbles, in
  passing, a spark
Struck out by a steed flying fearless
  and fleet;
That was all! And yet, through the
  gloom and the light,
The fate of a nation was riding that
  night;
And the spark struck out by that steed
  in his flight
Kindled the land into flame with its
  heat.

Considering his background, there can be no surprise that Paul Revere volunteered to warn the rebels of the coming of British troops. He was born in 1735 and became a silversmith of great repute whose craftsmanship was second to none in his home town of Boston. He was equally renowned for his support of the movement that was expressing growing discontent with British rule.

Revere and many other patriotic Americans believed that they no longer needed British protection now that the Seven Years War was over and the French threat from Canada dispelled. They also bitterly resented the imposition of new taxes and the enforcement of old ones by the British Government.

Their slogan, 'No taxation without representation,' indicated that they claimed their own elected Parliament in America and their own system of taxation.

Paul Revere was amongst the most active of the critics of the British Government. Following the so-called 'Boston Massacre' of 1771, in which British soldiers fired upon a mob and killed three of them, he had used his skill as a craftsman to cut copper plates to commemorate the event, and had staged an exhibition in his house in the old North Square of Boston. Later he played a prominent part in the 'Boston Tea Party', and had been employed to ride to New York with the news of the incident by the local Committee of Correspondence.

These Committees, founded in 1772 by Samuel Adams, were responsible for writing news-letters and distributing them throughout the colonies by means of post-riders. It was understandable that Paul Revere, as one of the finest horsemen in Boston, was willing to act as a post-rider.

The spreading of news and the emergence of provincial congresses or revolutionary parliaments steadily increased the rebellious feelings of the Americans, who began to arm themselves. Each colony had its own volunteers or militia and established companies of Minute Men, so named because they were civilians who were

Below: Paul Revere's ride from Charleston to Lexington, from the painting by Robert Reid (1862-1929) in the Massachusetts State House, Boston.
RADIO TIMES HULTON PICTURE LIBRARY

prepared to take up arms in an instant.

General Gage, the Governor of Boston, had lived for eighteen years in the American colonies and had married an American. He hoped that he could act peacefully to calm down the situation, but to his dismay opposition to the British was not confined to Boston and Massachusetts, but rapidly spreading south to other colonies. Alarmed at the reports of growing stores of arms and ammunition accumulated by the Americans at Concord, some twenty-five miles from Boston, he decided to take preventive action and raid the town early one morning before the country-side was awake.

Unfortunately for him, the news of the supposed surprise raid leaked out, as the troops that he intended to use were quartered in Boston. In order to save the stores at Concord and at neighbouring Lexington, and to warn Samuel Adams and another patriotic American, John Hancock, of General Gage's plans, the Boston Committee of Correspondence chose two men to raise the alarm along the roads from Boston to Lexington and Concord. One of these men was William Dawes, the other Paul Revere.

By mid-afternoon on 18 April Paul Revere had heard in his silversmith's shop of General Gage's intention, but neither he nor Dawes was certain about the route that the British troops would take. In those days Boston was connected to the mainland by a thin isthmus called Boston Neck. The troops could march out across the Neck and then, having taken the coast road to Cambridge, advance towards Lexington either by the northern route or via Waltham. Another alternative was for the troops to be ferried across the River Charles to East Cambridge.

The previous Sunday Paul Revere had ridden to Lexington and on his way home had stopped at Charlestown. There he had arranged a signal code with the leader of the Committee of Safety: 'if the British went out by water, to show two lanterns in the North Church steeple; and if by land, one as a signal, for we were apprehensive it would be difficult for us to either cross the River Charles or get over Boston Neck.'

Revere's main problem was that the British knew him to be a patriotic express-rider, and consequently at such a time might have him closely watched. However, all went according to plan. Dawes slipped through a British patrol and set off via Brookline and Cambridge.

Revere persuaded two friends to row him across the river in a boat he had kept especially for the purpose, confirmed with the Charlestown Committee of Safety that the signal from the church steeple had been seen, borrowed a horse which was considered the fastest and strongest in the area, and turned in the direction of Concord. On such a horse, under a cloudless sky on a moonlit night, he expected to reach Lexington to warn Samuel Adams in less than an hour, for it was only a distance of eleven miles.

As he left Charlestown he espied two British officers, mounted and with pistols drawn. One raced towards Revere whilst the other blocked the road. Revere, hoping to avoid suspicion, turned his horse and headed back towards Charlestown. He knew that there was an alternative route open to him, and trusted that he would not be followed. To his dismay he noticed that one of the officers was galloping across a field to intercept his new route. Luck suddenly came his way for the officer's horse slipped in soft mud and before he could extricate himself Paul Revere had galloped away.

By midnight he was in Lexington, where he gave news of General Gage's plans to Adams and Hancock, rested his horse and took some refreshment. Whilst he was telling his friends the news Dawes arrived safely. There was a shortage of horses in Lexington and consequently both express-riders decided to speed onwards with their existing mounts who seemed comparatively fresh.

On the journey to Concord, whilst Dawes and Dr Samuel Prescott, who had joined them, were alarming a household, Paul Revere saw two British officers riding along the road ahead of him. Thinking he could capture them with the help of his compatriots, he gave chase. Unfortunately he found himself the pursued instead of the pursuer, for other officers came out of the woods. Revere spurred his horse onwards, but the animal was now finding the strain of the night ride too much, and was leg-weary and near exhaustion. Revere was quickly captured although Dawes and Prescott, seeing the state of affairs, set their horses at a stone wall and had departed before the British had time to realise what was afoot.

The British interrogated Revere in the most gentlemanly fashion, and he answered their questions truthfully. Such was the behaviour between some captors and prisoners in the eighteenth century! He was ordered to mount his horse but, knowing his reputation as an express-rider, one of the officers took the reins from his hands with the remark 'By God, sir, you are not to ride with reins' and ordered another to lead the horse. An hour later, when the party had reached the outskirts of Lexington, Paul Revere was set free although his horse was retained.

Amazed at his good fortune, Revere walked back across the fields to the house where Adams and Hancock awaited him. After animated discussion it was agreed that the British troops might arrive at any moment, and consequently those who feared for their lives left the house and hid in the nearby woods. Paul Revere went with them, but later returned to the house to collect a bundle of incriminating papers. By now the entire neighbourhood knew of the imminent arrival of the British, and the rebellious Americans had made the necessary preparations at Concord to receive them.

It was five o'clock in the morning before the British troops reached Lexington, where they were confronted on the Green by the local Minute Men. Probably no fighting was desired by either side, but it was perhaps inevitable that shooting should start. Major Pitcairn ordered the Americans to disperse, they refused and eighteen were killed or wounded before they gave way. The British then marched to Concord and reached their objective, but the raid achieved next to nothing and after another skirmish the troops were ordered to march back to Boston.

You know the rest. In the books you
   have read
How the British Regulars fired and
   fled,
How the farmers gave them ball for
   ball
From behind each fence and farmyard
   wall,
Chasing the Redcoats down the lane,
Then crossing the fields to emerge
   again,
Under the trees at the turn of the road,
And only pausing to fire and load.

Many in the British Government, including the King, did not share Chatham's understanding of the need for the growing independence of the Americans. Given their attitude, it was perhaps inevitable that war should eventually develop, and that Boston should be a breeding ground for discontent. And because the war did start following the disastrous raids on Lexington and Concord, and because Paul Revere has always symbolised the idea of resistance to the continued British rule, it is right that his memory should have been immortalised by Longfellow:

For borne on a night wind of the past
Through all our history to the last,
In the hour of darkness and peril and
   need
The people will waken and listen to
   hear
The hurrying hoof-beats of that steed
And the midnight message of Paul
   Revere.

The Retreat from Moscow

In 1807 Tsar Alexander I of Russia signed a treaty of peace at Tilsit with Napoleon. Three years later, disgruntled at the Emperor's territorial gains in Prussia and Poland, and insulted by the news of his marriage to the daughter of the Austrian Emperor, the Tsar began re-opening trade negotiations with Britain. Such action did not appeal to Napoleon whose thoughts turned to the invasion of Russia, whilst in his dreams of fantasy he envisaged himself as the conqueror of all Asia.

In the late spring of 1812 he began to mass his Grande Armée, conscripting 120,000 Frenchmen to whom were added more than 400,000 recruits from Germany, Austria, Poland and Italy, all of whom vowed to follow his eagles and standards. Only Sweden, of all Continental nations, failed to be mesmerised by the glory of his past achievements.

In May he arrived at Dresden where many of the European Kings and Princes paid him homage. To them he announced that he intended to destroy the Tsar within five weeks. To his soldiers he proclaimed: 'Russia is dragged by her Fate. Her destiny must be accomplished, let us march; let us cross the Niemen; let us carry war into her territory.'

When his army crossed the river Napoleon decided to explore the river banks. As he did so his horse stumbled and he fell to the ground. 'A bad omen – a Roman would return home' one of his staff declared. Napoleon should have heeded the omen.

By mid-August the French army had reached Smolensk, despite the stupendous problems of ever-lengthening lines of communication and supplies which were under constant attack from the Cossacks. A month later, after an indecisive battle at Borodino, the Grande Armée reached Moscow. Napoleon's belief that the occupation of the city would result in the Tsar pleading for peace was rudely shattered. It was as though no one, least of all the Russians, cared for the fate of Moscow. Napoleon's prize literally turned to ashes before his eyes, for the day after his arrival much of the deserted city was destroyed by fire.

The Emperor stayed for five weeks in Moscow before giving the order to leave the city whose capture had proved so fruitless. He intended to lead his remaining 115,000 troops to the Ukraine, but the Russians under General Kutuzov blocked his retreat, compelling him to retrace his steps along the route by which he had entered Russia. This route had been ravaged, with villages in ruins, the earth scorched and the autumn harvest destroyed.

Before Smolensk was reached, a distance of 200 miles, the first freezing snows of the winter began to fall. The mornings were heavy with frost and the early evenings shrouded by choking fog. Napoleon rested for five days in Smolensk before ordering his army to march back to Europe. 'March' was a ludicrous word, for his dispirited and ill-disciplined soldiers hardly had the strength to put one foot in front of the other.

His horses, ill-fed for months, were in no state to withstand the rigours of winter and died in their thousands. No sooner were they dead than the rabble of the army, starved beyond measure, cut them up to use their skins for protection against the cold and to drink their blood. Each night many of the soldiers collapsed in sleep, to be frozen to death before dawn.

Hounded by the Russian troops who mercilessly annihilated the stragglers of an army, which stretched from vanguard to rear-guard for fifty miles, it seemed that the entire Grande Armée would be destroyed before it left Russian soil. Only the brilliant generalship of Napoleon at the battle of Beresina prevented such a catastrophe. Eventually 10,000 troops, the remnants of an army, reached Prussia, abandoned by their Emperor who had returned to Paris to disprove rumours of his death.

Above, right: **The retreat from Moscow;** painted by Adolphe Yvon, engraved by Jonnard.

Right: **Retraite de Moscou by C. Delori.**
ALL, MARY EVANS PICTURE LIBRARY

Following spread: **Retreat from Moscow,** from a painting by Meissonier.
GILLES LAGARDE

The Battle of Hanau

By 1813 Napoleon was showing signs of decline and although his manner was still regal his reputation for infallibility was on the wane. In May of that year after the Battle of Lutzen he confided to one of his generals: 'My eagles are again victorious but my star is setting'. In the battles he was now fighting there was a grumbling discontent among his senior commanders and being not unaware of their mood he had remarked that it was not his army which wanted peace but his generals! The 'big epaulettes' were loud in complaint of their distaste for life in bivouacs when the luxury of the estates the Emperor had bestowed upon them beckoned.

His adversaries, on the other hand, had learnt much and had changed the whole character of war against him. Encouraged by the examples of Spain and Russia, whole nations opposed him with vast armies who fought with a spirit and enthusiasm inspired by their common nationality. For this reason Leipzig was justly called 'The Battle of the Nations' and it was at this battle, where he was so badly served by both his commanders and his cavalry, that the climax of his decline came about, the French losing hold on Germany and their military.

Napoleon was still a great commander, however, and though outnumbered, succeeded in getting away from Leipzig with some 80,000 of his troops. By 28

October 1813, he had reached the vicinity of Hanau on his way to Frankfurt, the allied armies in pursuit but unable to overtake him. They hoped, however, that General Wrede would be able to intercept him and cut off his retreat to Frankfurt.

Wrede was a complex character who had been made a count by Napoleon and also owed his military advancement to him. He had been a lawyer before joining the army and had risen rapidly to command the Bavarians and an Austrian Corps who had joined the allies in October. His force included some 10,000 cavalrymen. After forced marches from Braunau and a controversial besieging of Wurzburg, he moved north-west to Aschaffenburg where he learnt that his opponents were retreating through Fulda, fifty miles to the north.

Wrede chose Hanau, on the great post-road from Fulda to Frankfurt, as the place where he would block the French retreat. Hanau was then a town of some 15,000 inhabitants situated between the Rivers Main and Kinzig. The Kinzig, especially in the rainy autumn of that year, was a serious obstacle, passable for all arms only at the Lamboi Bridge north-west of Hanau.

Napoleon heard of Wrede's arrival at Hanau and decided to outflank him by using an old road through the forest to the north of the town. Wrede panicked, moved across the River Kinzig and deployed his army in hastily selected and unfavourable positions which were so bad as to justify Napoleon's later remark that although he had been able to make Wrede a count he had failed to make him a general! Wrede would have done better to hold the Kinzig gorge at Gelnhausen further east. At this stage, however, he had no idea that he was opposing his former mentor, and was under the impression that only part of Napoleon's army was against him.

With the River Main at his rear and the Kinzig to one flank Wrede now faced thick woods which concealed the approach of the French! On 30 October, Macdonald's corps and eighty cavalier squadrons under Sebastiani determined to win what they could at the sword's point, attacked Wrede's left and drove them off the field of battle.

The French guns now attacked Wrede's centre and pushed their cavalry against it. Eventually Wrede's troops were forced to retreat but the Kinzig prevented them doing so directly and they were compelled to move to the left. They suffered heavily, thousands being driven into the Kinzig and drowned. Seeing the danger to his left and centre Wrede tried to bring two brigades from his right to help but in the confusion they were pushed onto the Lamboi Bridge which was insufficient for their passage and again the Kinzig claimed several hundreds drowned.

That night, a much chastened man, Wrede bivouacked with his right on the Lamboi Bridge and his centre and left along the Aschaffenburg road and holding Hanau. Napoleon had no desire to pursue him and continued his retreat on Frankfurt leaving a rear-guard to stop Wrede interfering with the remainder of the army still behind.

On 31 October, Hanau was bombarded, Wrede evacuated it but with the French occupying the town and blocking Lamboi Bridge, he was powerless to prevent Napoleon's remaining troops passing along the road beyond. Stung to the quick he advanced yet again, failed, and was badly wounded. In four catastrophic days from 28 to 31 October he had lost 9,250 officers and men and Napoleon had safely slipped through the net.

The Battle of Hanau was a dignified termination to the exploits of the French revolutionary army beyond the Rhine and threw a parting ray of glory over their long and successful career.

Left: The Battle of Hanau, a painting of the Battle by Emile-Jean-Horace Vernet.
NATIONAL GALLERY, LONDON

The Battle of Waterloo

Many reasons have been given for Napoleon's defeat at Waterloo by an army that was smaller and of very mixed quality. But nothing contributed more to the failure than Marshal Ney's handling of the attacks, and in particular his handling of the French cavalry. Ney was rightly regarded as one of the staunchest and bravest of Napoleon's marshals, but his tactical blunders at Waterloo were fatal for France.

The Duke of Richmond gave a magnificent ball in Brussels on the evening of 15 June. Before the ball ended senior British officers quietly left to rejoin their regiments. The following afternoon the citizens of Brussels heard the noise of gunfire from the direction of Quatre Bras, twenty miles to the south. There Marshal Ney was defeating an inadequate Netherlands force who were defending the cross-roads which linked communications between the Prussian and allied armies. Meanwhile, six miles away at Ligny, Napoleon was assaulting the Prussians under Field-Marshal Blücher and forcing them to retreat.

On the morning of 17 June Napoleon detached 33,000 troops under Marshal Grouchy to pursue the Prussians, whilst he prepared for his titanic strugle with the Duke of Wellington. By nightfall torrential rain and thunderstorms had turned the surrounding countryside into a quagmire. The soldiers in both armies were drenched, and spent a singularly uncomfortable night. The Emperor slept at Le Caillou, a farmhouse about two miles from Wellington's armies. He breakfasted at eight o'clock and told his staff that he intended to dine that night at the Palace of Laeken in Brussels. An hour later he mounted his horse and rode forward to inspect the opposing army.

Napoleon's first major attack had been repulsed by the steadiness of Picton's infantry, extended in line, and the vigour of the English light cavalry under Lord Uxbridge, although the cavalry rashly continued their charge deep into the French lines, and consequently lost a quarter of their precious number. Napoleon then prepared another major frontal assault and ordered Ney to start by clearing the outpost of La Haye Sainte.

Whilst the attack on La Haye Sainte was being pushed home Ney thought he saw the whole English line over the crest begin to retreat. In fact it was withdrawing only a matter of yards and generally closing up. Ney, however, was convinced that the English were beaten and he launched a major cavalry attack to take advantage of their apparent flight. As the masses of French cavalry trotted up the slope the English guns were galloped up to the front line to take

their place between the squares into which the infantry now formed.

Captain Mercer's nine-pounders were presented with opportunities of slaughter. In his own words, 'The discharge of every gun was followed by a fall of men and horses like that of grass before a mower's scythe'. And when by sheer force of numbers the French cavalry did overrun the guns, whose gunners in most instances took refuge in the neighbouring infantry squares, they did not spike the guns or tow them away, but rode helplessly round the red-coat squares looking in vain for an entry.

To launch cavalry against unbroken squares was always a tactical blunder, yet Ney persisted. Five times in two hours the cavalry recoiled from the attack, and five times they re-formed and renewed their expensive and futile attempts. And then, to make matters worse, at approximately five p.m. Kellermann's cavalry, which had been waiting in reserve, were also called into the attack. Nine thousand of the cavalry, it has been estimated, were jammed into a front only eight hundred yards wide, and still the English guns mowed them down, and still the squares held.

In a sense it was stalemate, although a stalemate expensive to the French. The English could not clear the French from their lines, once they were there, and the guns temporarily abandoned, because they had too few cavalry themselves, as a result of their earlier over-eager attack. But by five o'clock the first Prussians had already arrived.

Later Ney did change tactics and came within minutes of breaking the English line by a combined infantry and cavalry attack, but Napoleon crucially delayed launching his Old Guard and the English survived long enough for the Prussians to enter decisively and sweep away the exhausted French army.

Above: 'On the Eve of the Battle of Waterloo' by E. Crofts.
WALKER ART GALLERY, LIVERPOOL

Overleaf: 'An Incident at Waterloo' by Richard Beavis.
RICHARD GREEN GALLERY, LONDON.
PHOTOGRAPH: RODNEY TODD-WHITE AND
SON

The Battle of Balaclava

When the Russian cavalry first threatened the British base at Balaclava during the Crimean War, they were opposed by only a handful of Highlanders under the command of Sir Colin Campbell. Yet these men by themselves drove off the leading squadrons of the Russians.

Shortly afterwards the Heavy Brigade under General Scarlett, on their way to help Campbell, rode directly across the front of 3,000 Russian cavalry. Scarlett immediately wheeled his 700 men into line to face the oncoming enemy and, astonishingly, the Russians halted. Scarlett, apparently ignoring this invitation to charge, continued to dress his lines with infinite care and patience; then, satisfied at last, he ordered his trumpet to sound the charge and leading his first line by fifty yards disappeared into the mass of the Russians. He was followed by three successive waves of the Heavies, all pounding furiously uphill into the thick of the battle.

Then, miraculously as it seemed to Raglan and his staff watching from the plateau above, the red coats of the British, instead of being swallowed by the grey of the Russian mass, began to emerge on the other side, and the nucleus of the Russian formation began to break up and disperse. The Russians were in retreat.

The Light Brigade were waiting only five hundred yards away, impatient and eager to take part in the battle. But Lord Cardigan, now safely arrived from his yacht where he slept at night, would have none of it. Not only would he not attack in support of the Heavies, he would not order the pursuit of the disconcerted and retreating groups of Russian cavalry. And so the Russians escaped without further trouble, the Heavies being too exhausted to pursue them – and the chance of a famous victory for the combined cavalry brigades vanished.

There was little chance of Cardigan working constructively with Lord Lucan, who was both his brother-in-law and his direct superior as Commander of the Cavalry Division, and the action that did ensue became famous for its futility and senseless bravery. Lord Raglan, looking down from the plateau, saw that the Russians were about to tow away the English guns on the Causeway Heights from the redoubts which had been abandoned at the very beginning of the action. Raglan then issued his famous fourth order, instructing Lucan 'to advance rapidly to the front and try to prevent the enemy carrying away the guns'. To complete the tragic muddle he gave the message to Captain Nolan, who detested Lucan.

Lucan could not understand Raglan's order. Nolan in his impatience could not or would not explain it clearly, and

Lucan and Cardigan were not sufficiently on speaking terms to discuss its apparent dangerous absurdity. The result was that Cardigan led his cherished Brigade to certain destruction against the guns at the end of the North Valley and not, as Raglan intended, to recover the British guns on the Causeway Heights. It seems miraculous that only 113 men were killed and 134 wounded. The 517 horses killed or wounded out of 673 indicates more accurately the odds that were faced.

The fact that the Charge is today considered to be one of the most glorious incidents in British military history is largely due to the popularity

of the epic poem written by Alfred, Lord Tennyson. The poem appealed to Victorian patriotism and was recited in every city, town and village throughout the land.

Half a league, half a league,
  Half a league onward,
All in the valley of Death
  Rode the six hundred.
'Forward the Light Brigade!
Charge for the guns!' he said:
Into the valley of Death
  Rode the six hundred.

Cannon to right of them,
Cannon to left of them,
Cannon behind them
  Volley'd and thunder'd;
Stormed at with shot and shell,
While horse and hero fell,
They that had fought so well,
Came thro' the jaws of Death,
Back from the mouth of Hell,
All that was left of them,
  Left of six hundred.

When can their glory fade?
O the wild charge they made!
  All the world wonder'd.
Honour the charge they made!
Honour the Light Brigade,
  Noble six hundred!

Above: The 6th Inniskilling Dragoons at the Battle of Balaclava.
NATIONAL ARMY MUSEUM, LONDON

Overleaf: 'All That Was Left of Them', a copy of a painting by R. Caton Woodville.
MICHAEL OSBORN

The Battle of Fuentes de Onoro

Early in March 1811 Massena, called by Napoleon 'the favoured child of victory', was compelled to begin his retreat from Portugal. It was the turning point of the Peninsular campaign, if not of the entire Napoleonic Wars. By April Almeida, the key gateway to northern Portugal, was the only strategic fortress still held by the invading French, but the food supplies of their garrison were low and they could not hold out for more than a few weeks. Wellington knew this and believed that Massena, now resting at Salamanca, would mount a relief and rescue operation.

His belief proved correct for on 1 May Massena, re-equipped and re-inforced, crossed the River Agueda at Ciudad Rodrigo with 45,000 troops. Wellington, with about 34,000 infantry and less than 2,000 cavalry, was prepared for his advance and had selected the small village of Fuentes de Onoro (Fountain of Honour), where the main road from Ciudad Rodrigo to Almeida crossed the River Dos Casas, as the position from which he would join battle. Massena had to cross the river, and the nature of the terrain made it virtually impossible for him to cross it either north or south of the village.

The French arrived on 3 May and a skirmish ensued as they attempted to wade through the river under a hail of bullets from Wellington's troops, which included Portuguese and Germans, hidden in the houses on the opposite bank. By sheer weight of numbers the French managed to gain a foothold before being driven back across the river. By nightfall the village still remained in Wellington's capable hands.

War in those days was more chivalrous than it was to become later, and on the morrow there was an uneasy truce as both French and English collected their dead from the village streets. Late in the afternoon some of the English even arranged a game of football. The same spirit months earlier had caused the French to return a greyhound to an English officer after it had pursued a hare across the French lines, and Wellington to send one of his officers with condolences after a French general had been shot through the nose.

Early on the morning of 5 May, 3,500 French cavalry, having made some preliminary explorations the previous evening, crossed the Dos Casas to the south-west of Fuentes de Onoro and successfully pushed back the British cavalry to the hamlet of Poco Vehlo. With the British seemingly unable to withstand the French cavalry, Massena launched a frontal attack on Fuentes, his troops advancing in their usual manner of three densely packed columns.

Wellington, worried at the turn of

events, ordered 'Black Bob' Crauford, possibly the most popular officer in the British army, to send in his troops as a support for the badly harrassed 7th Division. Crauford, who had only returned from sick leave in England the previous day, carried out his task brilliantly. The British cavalry, which included a regiment of Hanoverian Hussars, were heavily outnumbered but they kept on charging the French guns until their horses were exhausted and their riders almost dropping from the saddle with fatigue. Their gallantry prevented the French gunners from annihilating the British infantry.

Under Crauford's guidance the British infantry withdrew two miles to new positions with almost parade-ground-like precision. The French cavalry constantly attacked the British squares but they could not break them. At the height of the battle one pair of guns in

Major Bull's horse artillery seemed to have been submerged beneath hordes of French cuirassiers, but their commander, Captain Norman Ramsey, ordered the guns to be limbered up, and his gunners to draw their sabres.

'Suddenly', wrote William Napier, 'a thick dust arose and loud cries and the sparkling of blades and flashing of pistols indicated some extraordinary occurrence. The multitude became violently agitated, an English shout pealed high and clear, the mass was rent asunder and Norman Ramsey burst forth, sword in hand, at the head of his battery, his horses breathing fire, stretched like greyhounds along the plain, the guns bounded behind them like things of no weight, and the mounted gunners followed close, with heads bent low, and pointed weapons, in desperate career.'

All day there was fighting in Fuentes as the French forced their way into the streets chock-full of dead and dying. Inexorably they drove the British up the steep hill towards the ridge at the top of the village. There they were met by the Connaught Rangers and Mackinnon's brigade, who hurled them back into the devastation which had once been houses but now was no more than rubble littered with corpses. By the end of the day Massena had failed to dislodge Wellington from the village.

The following day Massena admitted defeat. He could not advance to relieve Almeida as the British under Wellington still blocked his path. However, he managed to get a message through to the senior officer in the beleaguered garrison fortress ordering him to blow up as much of Almeida as possible and escape back to the French lines. It was a difficult command to obey, but due to

Above: Norman Ramsay at Fuentes de Onoro: an incident in the Peninsular War. Painting by W. B. Wollen.
NATIONAL ARMY MUSEUM, LONDON.

Overleaf: Fuentes de Onoro, 5 May 1811, by R. Caton Woodville.
PARKER GALLERY, LONDON

the sheer incompetence of the British was successfully carried out.

Days later Wellington told his staff that he considered that the battle of Fuentes de Onoro was the most difficult operation he had ever been concerned in, and against the greatest odds. He added that if Napoleon had been present he thought that the British might have been beaten.

The British cavalry were insufficient to follow up the battle by a counter-attack but at least they had played a valiant part in preventing Massena from attaining his objective.

The Retreat from Kabul

To understand the events that led to one of the greatest defeats ever inflicted upon the British by an Asian enemy, when only one man was allowed to escape after the ignominious retreat from Kabul, we must go back briefly to the First Afghan War in 1839. This war had the object of erecting in Afghanistan a barrier against encroachment from the west and securing the independence of the country. For this purpose the British decided to restore the exiled ruler, Shah Shuja, in Kabul. This, they accomplished; but lack of enthusiasm for the Shah and general political intrigue resulted in half a dozen regiments being left in Kabul.

These units settled down to garrison duties and a life which followed the pattern similar to that of the Indian stations from which they had come. There was a racecourse and polo ground and the band played at dinner parties, balls, in the messes and at the clubs.

General Elphinstone commanded, but it was a post for which he was entirely unsuited and his incompetence and vacillation were undoubtedly responsible for the rapid deterioration which set in. There was 'much reprehensible croaking', as Lady Sale wrote in her memoirs. Insurrection by the Afghanistans broke out, conditions became severe and food was short. Grumbling became open and there was an air of disaster about every British attempt to right matters. Soon the occupation became untenable and Macnaghten, the Envoy, decided that negotiation for safe return to India was the only solution. In these negotiations it was resolved that the British troops should evacuate their cantonments within three days. In the short interval before their departure Macnaghten was murdered and the situation had become so hopeless that no attempt was made to avenge his death.

On a clear and frosty day, Thursday 6 January 1842, with nearly a foot of snow on the ground, the ill-fated withdrawal of some 4,500 fighting men and 12,000 followers began. The 4th Irregular Horse and Skinner's Horse were stationed with the advance guard, Anderson's Horse being in the main body and the 5th Cavalry in the rear guard.

Two and a half hours were needed to cover the first mile and a taste of what was in store came early with heavy firing and attacks upon the column. By 9 January conditions had become so desperate and casualties so heavy that it was agreed that the ladies should go back to Kabul as captors. On the evening of the twelfth General Elphinstone ordered the march to push on at all costs as further treachery was suspected. From this point on confusion reigned and in a reduced and demoralised column all discipline was at an end.

At this point, Major Bellew, acting as Quartermaster-General of the column mustered some forty mounted men as an advance guard, among them a Dr Brydon of the Army Medical Services. At daybreak on 13 January they discovered that all traces of those in their rear had disappeared. Then a dispute arose over the best route to take and the party split, Dr Brydon taking in his party seven officers and six soldiers. An enemy cavalry attack reduced the party to five. Three of these being well mounted went on, leaving Brydon with a Lieutenant Steer who soon gave up the struggle. Brydon was then attacked by a party of twenty men whom he charged with his horse's bridle in his mouth, cutting right and left as he went through them. He soon encountered another party and this time he had to prick the tired old horse to raise a gallop. In the charge he was fired upon and broke his sword leaving only about six inches in the handle. Getting clear, he found the shot had hit his horse, wounding him in the loins. Gamely, he carried on until he met five horsemen draped in red who he thought were his own cavalry. As they turned out to be Afghans he tried to get away but his horse could hardly move and they sent one of their party after him. This man made a cut at Brydon who lost the last bit of his sword from the hilt guarding himself. The Afghan rode at him again and, just as he was striking, Brydon threw the handle of his sword at his head, but the Afghan cut him over the left hand. Brydon stretched down to pick up the bridle and, thinking he was reaching for his pistol, the Afghan rode off. Brydon then discovered he had actually lost his pistol and was wholly unarmed and, with his horse wounded and almost unable to carry him, all energy forsook him. However, he was at his journey's end. A sentry at the Fort at Jellalabad looking towards Kabul saw a solitary white-faced horseman struggling on towards the Fort. The alarm was raised. The soldiers lined the ramparts and, looking out through unsteady telescopes, gazed with awe upon two gallant survivors who were no more than messengers of death, for when Brydon's horse was put into a stable it, too, lay down and never rose again.

Above: Major H. W. Bellew, who was assassinated during the retreat; a painting by an unknown artist.
NATIONAL ARMY MUSEUM, LONDON

Following spread: 'The Remnants of an Army — Dr Brydon and Horse'; a painting by Lady Butler.
NATIONAL ARMY MUSEUM, LONDON

The Battle of Little Big Horn

No other American battle is known better by name and less by fact than 'Custer's Last Fight' or 'Custer's Last Stand'.

George Armstrong Custer was a Major-General before his twenty-fifth birthday and was afraid of nothing, a quality that led to his being noted five times for gallantry for his attacks upon Lee in the Civil War. After the war he reverted to Lieutenant-Colonel and was given command of the 7th Cavalry. He was as often in the midst of trouble as he was in the thick of fighting for, although a stern disciplinarian to his men, he had a contradictory streak of insubordination towards his superiors, his career being dotted with controversies and courts-martial.

In 1868 it was decided that new tactics would be employed against the Indians, and that they would be attacked in their winter camps where they were snugly holed up, concentrated and immobile. In May of that year Colonel Custer led his regiment of some 600 men from Fort Abraham Lincoln across the Missouri River from Bismarck, North Dakota, on his last ride. He was in bad humour and out to redeem himself from sharp reprimands he had recently received from President Grant and General Sherman for impudent remarks he had made which reflected on Grant's brother.

The 7th Cavalry was part of a column, which, with two other columns, were to converge on the rebellious Sioux and Cheyennes south of the Yellowstone River in Montana. One of the columns, General Crook's, was repulsed by the famous leader and Sioux Warrior, Crazy Horse. Crook returned to base but knowing nothing of this the other two columns met at the confluence of the Rosebud and Yellowstone Rivers and decided to send the 7th Cavalry to follow an Indian trail leading to the Big Horn Mountains and to then wait at a point on the Little Big Horn River for the rest of the force and a concerted attack.

At dawn on 25 June, at the rendezvous ahead of his schedule, Custer's scouts told him that about 10,000 Sioux and Cheyennes and 3,000 warriors under Chiefs Gall, Sitting Bull and Crazy Horse were ahead of and also behind him. He was faced with the alternative of letting them go or fighting alone. He had never shirked a fight and with a burning desire to erase his recent humiliation was in no mood to do so now. He led his regiment on to the west until, twelve miles from the river, he sent a detachment off to the south and left to scout for Indians. He also sent another detachment of three companies under Major Reno to the left across a tributary of the Little Big Horn River to ride parallel with his own column towards the west. Another company was

sent to the rear to guard the pack train which carried the ammunition and had fallen behind. After they had gone about nine miles Custer ordered Major Reno, one of his commanders, to recross the river and for the two columns to ride side by side. Soon scouts reported that the Indian encampment lay ahead across the Little Big Horn River. Custer ordered Reno to cross the river again and to charge the Indian village, promising close support when seen. He followed Reno for a while then turned off obliquely to the right to be lost to sight, a tactic he had used successfully before.

Reno forded the river and galloped towards the village. When mounted

Indians poured from the village Reno looked around for the promised help, but saw it was not forthcoming. He dismounted his men and took shelter in a small wood. As the Indians attacked him he decided to retreat back across the river losing half of his men and releasing the bulk of Indians from defending their village to mass against Custer approaching from a different angle.

Away to the right, climbing a hill, Custer at last saw part of the village ahead. Soon he was in action and the sound of battle roused Reno to order all the troops now under his command to move to Custer's assistance. This was difficult and too late, anyway. A wave of exultant braves, returning from the

massacre which had taken place in the village, pushed the little column back to the hill where they fought for their lives all through that day, the night and the next morning. Suddenly, in the afternoon the Indians moved off.

What had happened to Custer? No one will ever know. He was last seen galloping down a ravine towards the river. With his front blocked, the furious flank attacks by Chiefs Gall, Crazy Horse and Rain-in-the-Face probably sealed his doom. Nobody knows or ever will know exactly what happened. A horse, *Comanche*, was the sole survivor. Strangely enough the Indians could not have realised who Custer was as his body was not mutilated.

Above: 'Custer's Last Stand' by Edgar S. Paxson.
BY COURTESY OF BUFFALO BILL HISTORICAL CENTER, CODY, WYOMING: WESTERN AMERICAN PICTURE LIBRARY

Half of his regiment of 600 men and some 319 horses were lost, the action making an emotional impact on the American public as great as Balaclava did on the British.

The reason for his defeat? No one knows, but one of his gallant captains was certainly right when he said: 'We were at their hearths and homes – and they were fighting for all the good God gives anyone to fight for'.

The Battle of Omdurman

In 1898 the British, who at the time were rulers of Egypt, were forced to send an army from Egypt into the Sudan to subdue the Dervishes. This sect of Moslem fanatics, under their leader the Mahdi, had captured Khartoum and murdered General Gordon thirteen years earlier, and were now preventing the building of a transcontinental railway from Cairo to the Cape of Good Hope which was planned by Britain. The crucial battle of Omdurman took place on 2 September.

Sir Herbert Kitchener was certain that he could win the battle of Omdurman because he knew that the Dervish army, however numerous and fanatical, could never survive the accurate and sustained fire of the many Maxim machine-guns which the British possessed. And so it was. The Dervishes launched three separate and powerful attacks on the Anglo-Egyptian army, but each was destroyed before fighting could develop at close quarters.

The machine-gun was to continue to dominate the battlefield in the First World War, and in particular was to eliminate the possibility of the cavalry charge. But curiously enough the battle of Omdurman included an English cavalry charge that has become famous; not least because Winston Churchill, who was present with the English army both as a subaltern and as special correspondent for the *Morning Post*, took part in it and has vividly described the action in his books.

Kitchener was eager to prevent the enemy from retreating into Omdurman. He was confident that he could destroy them in the open, but did not relish the idea of street-fighting. He therefore ordered the 21st Lancers, during a pause in the battle, to reconnoitre the plain north of Omdurman to discover whether the way was clear for the English to enter the city.

The Lancers were trotting cautiously south when they were fired upon at close range by a small force of Dervishes lying in full view on their right. In answer to this threat the Lancers immediately turned into line and, acting in response to the shrill calls of the trumpet, charged. When they were only yards from their objective there suddenly arose from the desert several thousand more Dervishes, who had been concealed in a depression

Below: Detail of the standard bearer from the 'Flight of the Khalifa, after his defeat at Omdurman' painted by R. Talbot Kelly. WALKER ART GALLERY, LIVERPOOL

in the ground; a long line of men, ten or twelve deep, awaited the lances of the charging cavalry. The Lancers had no option but to ride straight at this sudden apparition.

Churchill, who himself used a pistol rather than his sword, survived the impact, and found his way through to re-form with his troop beyond; but others were not so fortunate. Bravely as they fought – and three Victoria Crosses were awarded for this one action alone – not all the Lancers could penetrate the human wall of Dervishes. Here no machine-gun could help the English, and in hand-to-hand fighting they had no advantage.

At the end of the battle it was estimated that Kitchener's army had lost only forty-eight killed, and 434 wounded, whilst 11,000 corpses of Dervishes were counted on the battlefield. Yet, in an action lasting only about five minutes, the 21st Lancers had five officers and sixty-five men killed or wounded and lost 120 horses. Within minutes the Lancers had taken up position to enfilade the Dervishes and, using their

Above: Charge of the 21st Lancers; detail from the painting by E. Matthew Hale.
MARY EVANS PICTURE LIBRARY

Overleaf: The Charge of the 21st Lancers; detail of the painting by Richard Caton Woodville.
WALKER ART GALLERY, LIVERPOOL

carbines now rather than their lances, scattered the enemy into the surrounding desert.

The charge was only a small incident in a major battle but its very incongruity sharply illustrates how much matters had changed since the Crimean War.

The Battle of Maiwand

The history of Afghanistan in the years 1878–80 was a chapter of violence, treachery and murder. The situation was not improved in 1879 when there was famine in India, crops failed, cattle died from foot and mouth disease and whole villages were wiped out by cholera.

In Kabul, the capital of Afghanistan, British residents were massacred during August and native troops mutinied. Seething unrest prevailed for the remainder of the year, particularly after nearly a hundred of the mutineers were tried and executed.

One of the most treacherous of the Afghan leaders was Ayub Khan, the Governor of Herat. By the spring of 1880 he had secretly entered into agreement with some of the local *sirdahs* (chieftains) and began to march across the mountainous countryside towards Kandahar at the head of an army of 1,000 regular cavalry, 4,000 other horsemen and more than 30,000 warriors.

Uncertain of the strength of Ayub Khan's army, but little dreaming that it was so vast, the British Commander-in-Chief ordered General Burrows to prevent Ayub Khan from reaching Kandahar, and if possible to compel the Afghan army to disperse by a show of force. Such orders showed a total lack of appreciation of the seriousness of the situation.

On 22 July spies reported to General Burrows that Ayub Khan had crossed the River Helmand and that his cavalry were patrolling the far bank. By the following morning the Afghan horsemen on their tough mountain ponies seemed to be everywhere, and skirmishes took place. Only in the evening did the magnitude of Ayub Khan's army become apparent to General Burrows and his staff.

At a hastily called council of war, some of Burrows' senior officers favoured a retreat towards Kandahar. Others advocated that the enemy should be shown a brave front. Whilst the officers were arguing, news was brought in by spies that Ayub Khan had occupied Maiwand on the Kandahar road.

The news left Burrows with only two options. He could retreat immediately or he could fight. Two vital factors had to be considered, but in the heat of the moment Burrows appeared to overlook them both. If he retreated at once it was doubtful if the Afghan cavalry and horsemen would pursue them, for they and their horses were exhausted after a long and arduous day in which some of them had travelled nearly fifty miles. If he fought he did so in the knowledge that he was without communications, at a distance of fifty miles from his base, without reserves or support, and with a desert at his rear. The one course he could not take was to entrench and await

the enemy attack. He decided to fight...

Dawn on 27 July found the British troops tired and jaded. The cavalry were worn out after excessive patrolling, and the infantry and camp-followers dispirited. The total strength of General Burrow's force was little more than 2,700 of which 600 were cavalry. Against them was a vast horde, many of them religious fanatics prepared to die in battle.

General Burrows decided to group his forces in the tiny hamlet of Mahmudabad, three miles from the fortified village of Maiwand. So hazy was the morning light that the British cavalry officers thought that the dark line ahead of them was trees. In reality the line was rank after rank of Afghan warriors.

By mid-morning thousands of enemy

horsemen and white-robed *ghazis* started advancing from Maiwand. Ayub Khan, seeing that his opponents were positioned in the walled gardens of Mahmudabad and were maintaining an area less than a third of a mile square, ordered his warriors to surround the hamlet and to rush in fearlessly on front, flanks and rear when the order was given. Within two hours many of the British had been slaughtered, but 'nothing could have been steadier or firmer than the conduct of all ranks of the cavalry during the very severe and trying cannonade to which they had been exposed whilst playing a passive part as escorts to the guns and protecting the flanks from the enemy's cavalry which literally swarmed round our left flank . . .'

The remnants of the British brigade were saved to some extent by nightfall. Under cover of darkness they managed to retreat. Guns were abandoned and many of the wounded left to the savage butchery of the Afghans. The cavalry did all in their power to help the stragglers, but their task was virtually impossible.

The following day, as the blazing sun rose higher and higher, the sufferings of the troops and the horses were appalling. Soldiers died of thirst clamouring for water, the transport horses and bullocks collapsed in their hundreds, and the transport treasure, including 60,000 rupees, was abandoned.

News of the disastrous defeat reached

Above: A battery of the Royal Horse Artillery and a detachment of the 66th Regiment.
ILLUSTRATED LONDON NEWS, 7 AUGUST 1880

Overleaf: 'Saving the Guns at Maiwand'; a painting by R. Caton Woodville.
WALKER ART GALLERY, LIVERPOOL

Kandahar by evening, stunning those who had imagined that General Burrows must have accomplished his mission without mishap. Kandahar was besieged until the redoubtable General Roberts relieved the city, after defeating Ayub Khan's army at Mazra. So was avenged the catastrophe of Maiwand – a battle at which the British cavalry had once again shown bravery and fortitude against overwhelming odds.

The Horse in Military Tattoo

Although mechanisation was beginning to usurp the place of the horse in the Army soon after the cessation of hostilities in 1918, the Cavalry spirit to be 'up and riding' was still in the hearts of many of those who had survived. Military minds were putting the horrors of trench warfare aside and their thoughts were turning to the pomp and pageantry of more spectacular achievements and the grace rather than the grimness of a soldier's life.

For some years a Torchlight Tattoo had been held at Aldershot; and, with 40,000 troops and 2,500 horses under command and military charities desperate for funds, the General Officer Commanding set his officers to work to display their artistic talent. They excelled themselves and soon the Tattoo had earned a cachet that bracketed it with the other great social events of the Season, particularly Royal Ascot, which like the Tattoo demanded the finest horses. The horses became essential actors in the pageantry required to tell 'our rough island story' and were called upon to play a large part in the history that was depicted.

In 1921 the 9th Field Brigade, Royal Artillery, took part in a Musical Drive which was to become a feature of future Tattoos. Every limber, every gun and every spoke of every wheel were outlined in a mass of red, white and blue electric bulbs so that the evolution of the performance could be followed even under the cloak of darkness. The precision with which these galloping six-horsed teams wheeled and counter-wheeled, weaving serpentine patterns, thrilled the crowds. Keeping strict time to the music, at one moment they seemed to be inextricably mixed before swinging clear and departing yet always threatening to come into collision, a skill developed only after constant practice.

Next, to the delight of the females in the audience, Sandhurst cadets performed a Musical Ride. The young Prince Charmings of the Academy put their hunters through various concerted movements at the trot, in pairs, waltzing and tangoing like professionals, while the cadets sang 'Land of Hope and Glory'. It was intended to introduce the 'Shimmy Dance', the hit of those years, into the Ride but in deference to a protest from the horses, who up to then had not seen the latest Paris version, the idea was abandoned. The fair sex acclaimed 'Aren't they darlings' and there were those present who swear they were referring to the horses!

Encouraged, the organisers, working on the principle that there is nothing the horse cannot do, with a fine sense of theatre introduced in 1922 a new feature – a section tent-pegging with flaming pegs and the jumping of burning fences.

It was admirably staged, not by fiery steeds as one reporter imagined but by beautiful bay horses of the 7th Dragoons.

In 1923 the venue was moved to a picturesque glade called Rushmoor, fragrant with pine and heather, where the arena had earlier been tenanted only by curlew and snipe. It was decided that the Mounted Bands should play classical music during the Musical Drive. They had reckoned without the Gunners' chargers, however, who would have nothing to do with it and had to be allowed to canter, trot and gallop to the strains of the then Top Two, 'Sweet Hortense' and 'I Ain't Nobody's Darling', proving that temperament was by no means the prerogative of humans!

But temperament or not, there was still no lack of demand for the horse. In 1924 the 13th/18th Hussars excelled themselves with a most picturesque feature, the plaiting of an illuminated maypole. A striking effect was secured when the horses, walking, trotting and cantering around the maypole, wound round it festoons of coloured lights, lacing the emerald turf with all the colours of the rainbow and proving that cavalry chargers could dance around a maypole as well as any May Queen and her attendant sprites. The dance had required much practice and rehearsal, but the intelligent cavalry chargers were so well versed in the intricate steps and movements that they went through the routine almost without touch of heels or bridle.

Although it was an annual event, there was no staleness about the Musical Drive and in 1925 the proud carriage of the horses' heads was spotlighted by small electric bulbs carried at their brows. The riders spurred them on to the gallop to the rousing tune of 'Bonnie Dundee', then on in perfect rhythm to a bewildering number of flashing movements. Men and animals appeared as phantoms, disembodied and free in spirit, then once more joined together in a joyous movement as if directed by the hand of some invisible choreographer.

Despite the fact that in 1926 a prominent newspaper's second leader lamented that a horse was becoming a rare sight in the streets, the Army continued to make its obeisance at the shrine of Pegasus and at the Tattoo that year the Musical Drive and The Charge of the Light Brigade, employing some 700 horses, were the highlights. The Drive was a glorious spectacle of dash and smoke; forty-eight horses and twenty-four men moved like the stars in their intricate and pre-ordained courses while the lively strains of the gaily-uniformed musicians, accompanied by jingling spur and accoutrement, and drumming hooves, set every pulse atingling and prompted one correspondent to write:

> How comes it Maecenas, that no soldier, whatever the arm in which he has served or how many years he endured the pulverulenta of horrid war, can witness without little spinal thrills guns galloping to music in many convolutions?

The Charge of the Light Brigade was one of the most dramatic items Rushmoor had seen. The cavalry were seen riding into action with light playing on the rich colours of their uniforms, flashing and sparkling on polished accoutrements and steel glinting in a hundred different places. At their head rode the arrogant Cardigan in the full dress of the 11th Hussars. Men and horses seemed to capture the exaltation of that moment before the action which symbolised the epitome of their existence, the charge. And in that small arena where their horses were urged to the utmost, with heads kept straight and well together, they created that atmosphere of sublime confusion bestowed by the battlefield, which was exemplified at Balaclava. The motif of this Tattoo was 'Sacrifice' and after a moment of darkness came the most moving scene of all; the return of the handful of survivors. The full sum of heroism had been deployed in an action lasting only minutes in which some 247 men and 517 horses were killed or wounded, recalling the famous words of the French General Bosquet: 'C'est magnifique, mais ce n'est pas la guerre. C'est la folie'. Folly it may have been but it was certainly magnificent.

The horse's place in the affection of the nation, as leisure companion, artiste in the arena and example of animal beauty and breeding, continued. The quality of the annual spectacle of the Tattoo had no equal. The inspired pageantry, thrilling movement and soul-stirring effects left an ineffaceable impression on all those who witnessed it, and, in the scenes depicted, full scope was always given to the superb discipline and wonderful horsemanship of the cavalry. There were 400 of them in the 1928 Tattoo. First there was the portrayal of Wellington's Hunt with the pack sent to Spain for relaxation behind the lines of Torres Vedras, with the Iron Duke himself and all his brilliant Peninsular staff mounted on their beautiful chargers and happy because a fox was abroad! Next, 300 mounted knights rode into the arena in a scene which touched upon the emotional and religious feelings of the audience. As the lights went up they saw Richard the Lionheart at the head of his crusaders exhorting his knights to arms, to release Christ's

birthplace from the crescent. As he addressed them there was a glimpse on the far horizon of Old Jerusalem and in the distance a fiery Cross, the symbol of Christianity, burst into being and remained standing as a magnet for the mounted Templars who, with spears couched, hurled themselves against Saladin and his Arab hordes.

In 1930 the call for horses ranged from those required for Light Cavalry evolutions to four troops of Light Dragoons. Mounts were also required for Queen Elizabeth reviewing her troops in the armed camp at Tilbury and for King George II, the last king to lead his army in person on the battlefield at Dettingen. It was in this show that two twenty-one-year-old army veterans also took part. *Peter* and *Punch* were cream horses who had seen active service in France, *Peter* showing a battle scar on his head to that day. Proudly they drew the coach bearing King Charles' Commissioners and went through their parts as befits horses who were invited into the officers' mess of their corps to respond personally to the toast 'Horse Transport'.

In 1931, with horses and gay uniforms steadily giving way to motor traction and overalls, it was increasingly important for the Army to continue to cut a figure in the other arts and to contribute to the gaiety of peace. The organisers, however, were firm in their belief that the horse was not a beast that had been discredited by evolution. Refreshingly, they reverted to what was perhaps the origin of cavalry and introduced Boadicea in her chariot with her daughters, leading her tribesmen against the dreaded Romans and emphasising that the spiritual element in mankind cannot be extinguished by force or cruelty. And by a happy coincidence, accentua-

ting the emphasis on the role of woman, the Tattoo was attended for the first time by the young Princess Elizabeth, then only the fourth lady in the land but already a princess who had reigned in the hearts of thousands of young people. Could it have been here that her own deep love for the horse was first fostered?

In 1933 a most colourful item was that which was heralded by the medley of hunting songs for 'Jorrocks at the Hunt'. A welcome breath of Surtees was brought to Rushmoor. The renowned Cockney MFH and his redoubtable huntsman, James Pigg, at the head of his field assembled outside the Cat and Custard to hunt the fox brought rounds of applause. Soapy Sponge, Lord Scamperdale and Lucy Glitters could be seen capering under the autocratic eye of Mrs Barrington, who graciously shared her barouche with the Master of Ceremonies of Handley Cross, Captain Miserimus Doleful. A delightful scene when all around was gay: 'men, 'osses and dogs'!

Next year the background for the Show was Hounslow Heath in the seventeenth century. As a unit of our fighting forces cavalry is almost as old as British history, but it was not until the last Stuart King sat on the throne of England that the idea of heavy cavalry was first conceived. James II undoubtedly enriched the splendour of the British Army when he raised the Light Dragoons and Dragoon Guards Regiments. The crowds saw him escaping from the duties of State and, with his Queen, inspecting the newly formed Regiments which were certainly the apple of the royal eye.

It was Jubilee Year in 1935 and 'The Spirit of Cavalry' was one of the themes of the Tattoo. Marching in time to

The Centre Road. Camp Aldershott.

Souvenir programmes of the Aldershot Tattoos 1907 and 1927. ARTHUR KIPLING

music, men and horses were superb. They wove mazes and unravelled them, and ended with a spectacular charge, the manoeuvre most dear to a cavalryman's heart, which had those in the grandstand shifting uneasily in their seats at the realism of it all. One witnessed the alpha and omega of partnership between horse and man which had endowed the British cavalry with their tremendous reputation. It was of interest that the regiments taking part in the Ride – The Queen's Bays, 3rd Carabiniers and 4th Hussars – had each completed 250 years on the British Army Roster at that time. It was a notable occasion, too, for another splendid veteran, *Old Bill*, an army horse foaled soon after King George V came to the throne. He went all through the war, was in the Jubilee Procession to St Paul's, wore the ribbons of Mons, the Victory, General Service, Long Service and Good Conduct Medals and had now returned to Aldershot to finish his days with The Queen's Bays, the regiment in which he had started his career. No horse box from London to Aldershot for this great trooper, however – the thirty-four miles was completed on foot and it was reported that the gallant old fellow arrived as fresh as paint!

In the battle scene in Coronation Year, 1937, even the howitzers of The Royal Horse Artillery were drawn by tractors, only small contingents of The Blues and The Royal Scots Greys sustaining the honour of cavalry. Bareback riders, performing circus tricks *à la Russe*, vaulted amazingly among the other athletes, and mounted musicians added to the majestic harmonies of the Massed Mounted Bands; but there was no disguising the fact that the days of the horse in the Army were numbered.

The cloud of doom on a partnership of man and beast that came down from the crusades brooded over the Tattoo. It was more than the fact of Coronation Year that made it appropriate for the last figure painted into the canvas to be that of an historical horseman of ancient chivalry – Dymoke, the King's Champion who no longer rode into Westminster Hall on Coronation Day but here at Rushmoor was still a brave figure, a champion who had performed his office in many ages and whose spirit was timeless.

The Tattoos continued in 1938 and 1939 but the shadow of the forthcoming war hung heavily about the Army. In 1939 the Royal Armoured Corps, comprising twenty ex-cavalry regiments, was formed and the care and attention once lavished on horses was now spent on tanks. The lights were going out at Rushmoor Arena and Military Tattoos there have never been revived. Yet it is natural that attention should be given to Aldershot to the total exclusion of other towns or cities where Tattoos have been, and are still being, held. This is no reflection on the excellence of those Tattoos. Edinburgh, York, Leeds, Tidworth, Cardiff and Colchester have fine traditions but they have not been able to emulate the standards set at Aldershot where there were vast resources of men, material and horses together with a large natural stage.

Mechanical traction has now completely taken over the Army in its professional duties but in the care of its men there is still a tradition of cavalry and the legend of the horse remains. The blood runs hotly at the memory of the spectacles in which this noble animal has played his part and taken his place alongside the British soldier. But, except for those of his kin who still wait upon the Sovereign, he no longer appears on the roll of the British Army where soldiers knew how a horse should look and how a horseman should look upon him.

He was a friend to those who served with him, and the regard the British Army held for this splendid animal is no better illustrated than in the order which was given at the end of a day's work or the return to stables when the lights went out at those spectacular Tattoos: 'Dismiss and make much of your horses'.

SHOT
O.1927.

Souvenir

The 3rd Light Dragoons

Nec aspera terrent – 'Neither do difficulties defer' – is an apt motto for a regiment which has been almost wiped out on more than one occasion but, phoenix-like, has risen again as undaunted as before.

The Queen Consort's Own Regiment of Dragoons was the junior of three regiments of dragoons authorised, along with troops of Life Guards and horse and regiments of foot guards and of infantry, by warrant in 1686. Dragoons were mobile infantry: they rode into action, leaving horses out of range, ten horses to a holder, while the regiment attacked in infantry formation.

The regiment first saw action in Ireland in 1689. It was to be almost annihilated fifty-four years later at Dettingen. The regiment was now 'The King's Own Regiment of Dragoons' in more than name: George II commanded his army in battle – the last British sovereign to do so. Losses were serious –

for the King's Dragoons 148 men and 191 horses – but, despite or because of royal leadership, the battle was won.

The regiment was on the left of the British line, plugging a gap between river and infantry, and thus was at the mercy of the French guns. Weakened by this barrage it was then charged by the pick of the enemy's cavalry, which outnumbered it by nine squadrons to two. By the time The King's Own Dragoons had charged the French twice only a quarter of their men were still in their saddles and two of the standards had been shot to pieces.

In about 1755 the Duke of Cumberland expressed strong feelings about the type of horse suitable for a dragoon:

His Royal Highness cannot approve the large footed, hairy legg'd Cart Horse that is too commonly bought for the Dragoons, by being ill chose; a Dragoon Horse should be from

Below: A private of the 3rd Light Dragoons by Major C. Hamilton-Smith, from 'The Costume of the Army According to the Latest Regulations 1814'.
NATIONAL ARMY MUSEUM, LONDON

Right: The 3rd Light Dragoons at the battle of Ferozeshah, 21 and 22 December 1845. 'Here fell more than 600 of Sir Hugh Gough's Army.'
NATIONAL WAR MUSEUM, LONDON

fifteen, to fifteen two inches, with light feet, and clean sinewy leg, well coupled and good filletts, no flat ribs, but even made with an oval Croupe, good thin Shoulders and nimble and active movers.

Light dragoons proved their worth in the Peninsular War, so in 1818 the 3rd (King's Own) Dragoons were converted to that role. In 1837 they embarked, 420 strong, for a tour of duty in India, where they soon earned their nickname, 'Moodkee Wallahs'. With the 4th Dragoons and some native cavalry they repelled the left flank of the Sikh army at Moodkee (1845). Small wonder that, four years later at Chillienwallah, the

Sikh cavalry bolted when they realised they were faced by their old foe; the British cavalry then found themselves attacking the enemy guns. The price of victory was high; out of the remaining 106 in the regiment, twenty-four were killed and twenty wounded.

In 1861 the regiment became hussars, so that it was as the 3rd (King's Own) Hussars that it fought in South Africa and in the First World War. However, they may have recalled their origins as mounted infantry with ironic amusement when, in 1915, Sir Douglas Haig ordered that each cavalry regiment should provide eight officers and 300 men for dismounted service in the trenches.

In 1934 the regiment was chosen for experiments in mechanisation. Despite initial lack of enthusiasm, and much heartache, its members finally decided 'to cooperate wholeheartedly'. But, for all their new role, the 3rd Hussars were still to suffer extremely severe casualties. Despite serious losses in the earlier, break-in phase of the battle of El Alamein (1942) they were ordered to push on through the enemy anti-tank and field-gun positions, to make a path for the breakthrough of further forces. General (later Field Marshal) Montgomery stressed the importance of the mission by saying that he was prepared to accept one hundred per cent casualties in men and equipment.

Above: Charge of the 3rd Light Dragoons at the Battle of Chillienwallah, 13 January 1849. NATIONAL ARMY MUSEUM, LONDON

The 10th Royal Hussars

The 10th Dragoons were raised in a matter of weeks in and around Hertfordshire to meet the threat of invasion by the Old Pretender in 1715. They missed him but came to grips with Bonnie Prince Charlie thirty years later, unsuccessfully at Falkirk and triumphantly at Culloden. Then, from 1758 to 1763, the regiment saw action in Germany.

In 1783, shortly after conversion to a light dragoon role, the 10th were awarded the title of the Prince of Wales's Own. This honour was soon made more than a mere formality. The Prince of Wales became Colonel Commandant in 1793 and took a great interest in the regiment's affairs. Perhaps it was this royal connection which attracted the dandy, Beau Brummell, who became a cornet in the 10th in 1795, only to resign three years later: the regiment was posted to Manchester and Brummell declared himself unprepared to go 'on foreign service'. In 1806 the regiment was converted to hussars. Hussar dress is a modification of Hungarian national costume. Although they had to wait until the following year for their hussar-pattern equipment it would seem that the 10th had adopted the more ornate foreign uniform as early as 1803.

A most remarkable event during the Peninsular War was the capture of an enemy general at Benevente in 1808 by Private Levi Grisdall. The Prince of Wales recognised this by promoting Levi to sergeant. At the evacuation of Corunna, cavalry regiments could embark only thirty of their six hundred or so horses and it was not until 1813 that the regiment was sufficiently rehorsed to return to the Peninsula. By now the 10th had an additional prefix, 'Royal', granted in 1813 by the Prince of Wales when Regent.

After the war in the Peninsula several of the 10th's officers denounced their commanding officer for lack of courage and mismanagement. Although a court martial cleared him of these accusations, the complainants were transferred to other units, so that it was with a very changed officer complement that the 10th fought at Waterloo.

In 1846 the regiment sailed for India, leaving its horses behind, as was the custom. Normally a newly-arrived unit would take over the horses of the regiment it was replacing. However, the 10th were going out not as reliefs but as reinforcements, so an advance party was sent out to find new mounts.

Of the first two hundred unbroken horses to reach the regiment's new quarters only fifty were Cape horses, bigger and seemingly stronger than the remainder, who were Arabs of more or less pure stock. However, it soon turned out that what the Arab lacked in size it made up for in endurance and spirit. These qualities carried a high premium. The Arabs, 'being all entire, gave a great deal of trouble by their indomitable spirits – biting, kicking and occasionally fighting with one another, both in and out of the ranks.'

In the 1860s the regiment adopted a non-pivot system of drill which, by cutting out several movements, resulted in greater speed of execution. The experiment aroused much discussion but, after various delays, was later officially adopted by the cavalry. The 10th again showed their inventive mettle by introducing, during Indian service in 1910, a new way of forming a machine-gun detachment which could get into action in only fifty seconds. The drill was adopted by the cavalry throughout India and was widely used during the First World War.

Meanwhile the 10th's association with the Prince of Wales continued. Queen Victoria's eldest son became colonel in 1863 and in due course his eldest son, the Duke of Clarence, was gazetted into the regiment, serving with it till his death while on leave in 1892. When Edward VII became King he kept up his association with the 10th as Colonel-in-Chief, a position retained by George V when he became King. The late Duke of Gloucester was commissioned into the 10th in 1919, and rose to the rank of major before he had to give up active service on the accession of George VI. The duke then became the regiment's Colonel-in-Chief.

Between times the regiment had fought in the Crimea and in Afghanistan; in the Sudan on horses borrowed from the Egyptian gendarmerie; and in Europe during the First World War. Although mechanised in 1936, the regiment was not fully equipped when it was rushed to France in 1940. There, in only three weeks, it lost all its tanks and suffered heavy casualties. By June 1941 it was posted, re-equipped, to North Africa and later went to Italy.

In 1969 the 10th Royal Hussars (Prince of Wales's Own) amalgamated with the 11th Hussars (Prince Albert's Own) to form The Royal Hussars (Prince of Wales's Own).

Right: An officer of the 10th Hussars circa 1850 depicted by Richard Simpkin (1850-1926), a volunteer officer known mainly for his military paintings.
NATIONAL ARMY MUSEUM, LONDON

Following spread: The 10th Hussars in India, Kirkee 1854; lithograph by E. Walker from a drawing by an officer in the regiment.
NATIONAL ARMY MUSEUM, LONDON

The Royal Scots Greys

Seventeenth-century Scotland was a crucible of disaffection and rebellion. Its inhabitants feared the imposition of episcopacy by England; ever since 1607, when James I forced a form of church service on unwilling Presbyterians, the Scots had been in ferment, and the issue was central to the outbreak of the Civil War. In 1678, to reduce growing civil disorder, Charles II ordered more troops to be raised there. Two independent companies of dragoons were recruited immediately, another troop was added four months later and after another three years a further three troops were authorised, the six to comprise a regiment of dragoons.

By 1694, when the regiment was sent to Flanders, it was mounted on grey or white horses and was soon nicknamed 'Grey Dragoons' or 'Scots Greys'. It was not until 1786, however, that the name gained official recognition when the title of the 2nd Royal North British Dragoons became also the 'Scots Greys'. The tag stuck: in 1877 the regiment's name was simplified to the 2nd Dragoons (Royal Scots Greys), which was reversed in 1921 to the Royal Scots Greys (2nd Dragoons).

The regiment had first been numbered the 2nd Dragoons in 1713; a board set up to report on regimental seniority admitted evidence that the Scots Greys had first crossed into England in 1685 to become the second regiment of dragoons on the English establishment.

The Scots Greys were engaged in Marlborough's principal battles. At Ramillies (1706) the astonishing secret of Trooper Christopher Walsh was uncovered by a surgeon tending the trooper's fractured skull: Walsh was, in fact, a woman. Her memoirs tell how she disguised herself, binding her breasts, to seek out her husband who had enlisted when drunk. She joined a foot regiment, was wounded at Landen and was taken prisoner a year later. On her release, she transferred to the Scots Greys and fought with them at Blenheim (1704). Whilst guarding some prisoners after that battle she spotted her husband *in flagrante delicto* with a woman camp-follower. The complexities of remonstrance and reunion overcome, she persuaded him to pass her off as his younger brother. After her sex had been discovered, she resumed her normal domestic role. When her husband was killed at Malplaquet, in 1709, her grief was extreme: she ate nothing for a week. This so excited the compassion of a Captain Ross that she became known throughout the army as 'Mother Ross'.

She remarried within months, but less than a year later this second husband was also killed in action. Back in England after the war, 'Mother Ross' was granted a pension of one shilling a day by Queen Anne. She outlived yet a third husband, and was herself buried at Chelsea in 1731, with full military honours.

At Dettingen in 1743 the Scots Greys captured a standard from the French Household Cavalry. But it was a subsequent trophy that was to be depicted on the regiment's badges and buttons: the eagle of the French 45th Regiment taken at Waterloo. Sergeant Ewart, the hero of this episode, was wounded in the groin while wresting it from a French ensign. He was then attacked by a lancer, but he deflected the lance with his sword, cutting the enemy's face from the cheek up. Next a foot soldier fired at him, missed and tried to bayonet Ewart who once again came out on top. He was rewarded with an ensign's commission in a Veteran battalion. When that regiment was reduced he was pensioned off at 5s 10d a day. He died in Manchester in 1854 and his body was reinterred at Edinburgh Castle earlier this century.

In the Crimea the Scots Greys took part in the charge of the Heavy Brigade under Brigadier-General Scarlett. This charge was infinitely more successful than the charge of the Light Brigade which has, ironically, been much more celebrated. In both the Boer War and the First World War the regiment dyed its

horses, not only as camouflage but also to hide the unit's identity. However, this practice was not kept up for long in the later conflict, as is evidenced by photographs taken later in the campaign showing the familiar grey horses.

The War Office wanted to mechanise the regiment in 1937, but opposition in Scotland was so bitter that a reprieve was granted. This proved only temporary: although the Scots Greys moved to Palestine a year later at six hours' notice with their horses, they were ordered to convert to an armoured regiment in May 1941. Five months later, they were in action in North Africa in their new role.

In 1969 the regiment was converted to armoured cars and amalgamation was on its way in 1971: union with the 3rd Carabiniers. A new regiment was born – the Royal Scots Dragoon Guards (Carabiniers and Greys).

A last triumph, although admittedly a more superficial one, was achieved by the Scots Greys just prior to amalgamation. Its regimental band recorded a traditional tune, 'Amazing Grace', which shot to the top of the hit parade and stayed there for a surprising number of weeks.

Facing page: Officer and trumpeter of the Scots Greys, circa 1884; a watercolour by R. Simpkin.
NATIONAL ARMY MUSEUM, LONDON

Below: The charge of 'Scarlett's 300' or Heavy Brigade at Balaclava; watercolour by Stanley Berkeley circa 1890.
NATIONAL ARMY MUSEUM, LONDON

Above: An artist's impression of the charge of the Scots Greys at Waterloo; oil painting by Lady Butler. LEEDS ART GALLERIES

The Royal Horse Guards

In August 1650 Sir Arthur Heselrigge, one of Cromwell's staunchest supporters, raised a regiment of horse, which by the following February was making a name for itself in Scotland and the West Country. When Charles II was restored to the throne, he replaced its Roundhead officers with Cavaliers. But he had hardly renamed it the Royal Regiment of Horse when Parliament disbanded the Army – and with it, this regiment. A month later, whilst the King was in Portsmouth, a revolt in London was successfully put down by two regiments still awaiting disbandment. The King hurried back to the capital to insist on the establishment of a standing force and so saved the British Army.

The Royal Warrant of 26 January 1661 put the reconstituted regiment of horse second only to the troops of Life Guards and put the Earl of Oxford at its head. Twenty days later, when he inspected the regiment, it was wearing blue coats, which happened to match Oxford's livery. In fact the men were probably still wearing the uniforms issued by Heselrigge which – a preserved standard suggests – were blue.

In 1685, the regiment was amongst those which defeated the rebel Duke of Monmouth, the eldest of the King's bastards, at Sedgemoor. When a more popular attempt was made on the throne by the Protestant William of Orange in 1688 some officers, unknown to the other ranks, tried to give the support of the

A drawing, circa 1814, by C. Hamilton-Smith when he was Deputy Quartermaster General.
NATIONAL ARMY MUSEUM, LONDON

Blues to the invader. The troopers discovered the plot in time and made their way back to James's camp where their loyalty was rewarded financially. But their allegiance was misplaced. James fled, William was placed on the throne, and the bloodless revolution was accomplished. Because the new King brought his own Dutch 'Blew Guards' with him the Royal Horse Guards gradually became known as 'The Oxford Blues'. In 1750 their nickname was officially adopted when their title became The Royal Horse Guards (Blue).

In 1689 the regiment fought side by side with the Life Guards in Flanders. From now on the two regiments' fortunes were to be closely intertwined. The Royal Horse Guards enjoyed a specially privileged position, compared with the cavalry of the line such as the horse and dragoons.

At the Battle of Warburg in 1760 the colonel of the Blues, the Marquis of Granby, lost his hat and wig in a charge and his bald pate did duty as a rallying point for his regiment. Hence comes the phrase 'going bald-headed at it', meaning rushing impulsively without counting the cost. Today the Blues are the only regiment whose men salute their officers when bareheaded; a custom that some claim stems from their bald colonel. Another explanation for the custom, however, dates from the beginning of this century when khaki forage caps were issued. The Blues did not

immediately receive cap badges. Rather than wear bare caps, they went about camp without them, in protest. And, to show they were as entitled to a cap badge as anyone, they continued to salute their officers.

In the 1760s the Blues were posted to Nottingham where they built themselves a riding school for £400. This was the first riding school in the Army, and served as a model for later ones.

The regiment performed outstandingly in Flanders against the French during the 1790s, perhaps prompting George III to order its posting to Windsor. George further consolidated his links with the regiment by frequently wearing its uniform and, in 1805, he presented its silver kettledrums. In 1812 the regiment formed part of the Household Brigade serving in the Spanish Peninsula.

The brigade was hastily reassembled on Napoleon's escape from Elba. By now the Duke of Wellington was its colonel and, either as a compliment to him or in recognition of their services at Waterloo, the Royal Horse Guards (The Blues) were granted the full status of Household Cavalry in 1820.

A composite Household Cavalry Regiment was formed for service in the Boer War, and again in 1914. R. J. T. Hills in *The Royal Horse Guards* (Leo Cooper 1970) describes the regiment's first shot in the Great War. A Blue was riding up a lane, rifle across his knee, towards a cottage. Suddenly a German

Above: Advance Guard Royal Horse Guards, Blues.
NATIONAL ARMY MUSEUM, LONDON

dashed out and jumped onto a bicycle. The Blue fired, hit the German and said to his companion, 'Well, I'll be damned. And I've been a third-class shot all my soldiering.'

The Blues narrowly escaped disbandment in the Army's reductions of the 1920s. Soon after the outbreak of the Second World War the regiment, still mounted, moved to Palestine, and it was not until 1942 that it was reorganised as an armoured car regiment. As such it fought in Italy.

In the meantime a Household Cavalry Motor Regiment had been formed at Windsor, raised from the Life Guards and Royal Horse Guards reserves. It took part in the invasion of Europe and was at the liberation of Brussels. One of the Blues' scout cars actually led the way into Holland.

Shortly before the end of the war this regiment was joined by the 1st Household Cavalry Regiment. Quickly unscrambling themselves after peace was declared, they resumed their identities as Life Guards and Royal Horse Guards (The Blues). But conversion to Chieftain tanks and amalgamation became inevitable. On 29 March 1969 the 1st Royal Dragoons joined the Blues to form The Blues and Royals (Royal Horse Guards and 1st Dragoons).

The 14th King's Hussars

The 14th King's Hussars acquired the nickname of the Emperor's Chambermaids in the Peninsular War by capturing a silver chamber-pot from the carriage of the escaped King Joseph Bonaparte, Napoleon's elder brother. The pot, soon known as 'the emperor', has been with the regiment ever since, almost as a mascot. The unit had landed at Lisbon in December 1808, and gained eleven battle honours during the Peninsular campaign.

The 14th Dragoons were hastily raised by Brigadier-General James Dormer in July 1715 to meet the threat of the first Jacobite Rebellion. The regiment fought the Old Pretender's forces at Preston, one of the few occasions when it was used in its correct dragoon role of mounted infantry. But, almost forty years later, during Bonnie Prince Charlie's invasion of England, it was used as cavalry instead. This refuted the Duke of Cumberland's assertion that:

the Dragoon Officers are to remember they are still Dragoons, and not Horse, that they are to march, and attack on Foot, if there is occasion when Dismounted, therefore the Men's Boots are not to be encumbered with great Spur Leathers and Chains, to hinder them from getting over a Hedge, Ditch or Works when they are ordered to Attack . . .

In 1776 the regiment was converted to light dragoon. It changed its head-dress and switched to a smaller horse, chosen for speed and nimbleness. Twenty years later the 14th became the Duchess of York's Own Light Dragoons because it escorted to London HRH the Princess Frederica, daughter of King Frederick William of Prussia and wife of George III's favourite son. The regiment gained the Prussian eagle as badge and its uniform facings went from lemon yellow to orange, the livery colour of the Prussian royal house.

The regiment was renamed the 14th King's Light Dragoons in 1830 after an inspection by William IV. He also gave the regiment permission to wear the royal cypher within the garter.

The regiment next saw action in India in the Second Sikh War, in 1848. And it was still in India ten years later, when the Mutiny broke out. It was then that Lieutenant Leith won the Victoria Cross, the first member of the 14th Light Dragoons to be so honoured. The tight-lipped citation states that James Leith 'charged alone, and rescued Captain Need of the same regiment, when surrounded by a large number of rebel infantry'.

Another Victoria Cross went to an officer of the regiment which was now the 14th (King's) Hussars, in the Second Boer War. This time the citation is more graphic:

On the 13th October 1900, at Geluk, when the enemy were within 400 yards, and bringing a heavy fire to bear, Major Brown, seeing that Sergeant Hersey's horse was shot, stopped behind the last squadron, as it was retiring, and helped Sergeant Hersey to mount behind him, carrying him for about three-quarters of a mile to a place of safety. He did this under heavy fire. Major Brown afterwards enabled Lieutenant Browne, 14th Hussars, to mount by holding his horse, which was very restive under the heavy fire. Lieutenant Browne could not otherwise have mounted. Subsequently Major Brown carried Lance-Corporal Trumpeter Leigh out of action.

Brown later super-added his mother's maiden name and as Edward Douglas Browne-Synge-Hutchinson commanded the regiment from 1907 to 1911. He also introduced the Regimental Medal, awarded annually to the member of the regiment who has contributed most in the year to the military efficiency or honour of the regiment.

In the First World War the 14th Hussars fought in Mesopotamia and in Persia. Coincidentally, the regiment followed almost the same steps in the Second World War before going to Italy. By then it had been amalgamated (in 1922) with the 20th Hussars to form the 14th/20th King's Hussars; conversion to a mechanised role came in 1939.

In 1947 the regiment adopted the arm-badge of crossed kukris. This was at the request of the 43rd Gurkha Lorried Brigade, to commemorate the units' close association in the Second World War. In 1969 HRH the Princess Anne was appointed Colonel-in-Chief.

Right: An officer of the 14th King's Hussars circa 1833, published by W. Spooner, London.
NATIONAL ARMY MUSEUM, LONDON

Following spread: Charge of the 14th King's Hussars at the Battle of Ramnuggur, 22 November 1848; engraved by T. Harris.
BY COURTESY OF THE 14TH/20TH KING'S HUSSARS

The 16th Queen's Hussars

'You will be mounted on the finest horses in the world, with superb clothing and the richest accoutrements.' This promise on posters proved very stimulating: fourteen months after being raised, in October 1760, the 16th Light Dragoons could report itself ready for foreign service. The following February a third of the regiment took part in the capture of Belle Isle, off Brittany. The remainder first saw action in Portugal in 1792, where they were conspicuous for dash and initiative.

George III took a great interest in the light dragoons: the first two regiments were raised at his command and, after several personal inspections, he honoured the 15th and 16th Light Dragoons with the titles 'King's' and 'Queen's' respectively.

The regiment next went to America where its success continued. On one occasion thirty men under a captain captured the American General Lee and his small escort. However, incessant action wore the regiment down and it was sent home in 1778.

The 16th The Queen's Light Dragoons distinguished itself by its service throughout the Napoleonic Wars. At Vaux in France in 1794 half the regiment charged a battery of nine guns supported by cavalry and infantry and carried off six guns and a howitzer. In Spain in 1811 five men, led by Sergeant Blood, charged the rear of a French squadron crossing a bridge, and took fifteen prisoners. And at Waterloo the regiment twice charged alongside the 12th, piercing through infantry squares, pursuing fleeing cavalry, and sabring the gunners at their pieces.

In 1816 the Duke of York, then Commander-in-Chief, announced to the regiment that it was one of four selected for conversion to lancer role. The lance had not been used by the British for some two hundred years but other armies had demonstrated its advantages over the sword at Genappe and Quatre Bras. It was suggested that lancer troops be attached to each cavalry regiment in 1811, but it was not until 1815 that fifty men of the 9th Lancers were trained to use the lance.

After a sea journey of just over five months the 16th The Queen's Lancers disembarked at Calcutta in 1822. Soon they were to be the first British troops to use the lance in action, at the siege of Bhurtpore in 1826. The regiment was now launched on a period of almost incessant warfare. In 463 days it covered 2,483 miles to Afghanistan and back. Conditions were severe and for some days the horses had to make do on a grain ration of 6 lb a day, for want of forage. The casualties in men were eighty-six. In horses, 233 were lost, 190 through starvation.

The picture on the following spread shows the regiment charging at Aliwal in 1846. Here fifty-eight of the 151 British dead and eighty-three of the 413 wounded were from the 10th Lancers. Seventy-seven of their horses were killed, thirty-five wounded and seventy-three were reported missing. The regiment fought in yet another major battle, Sobraon, in the same year, before returning to England. However, it was *au revoir* rather than goodbye: the regiment returned to India in 1865, and again in 1889. During the latter visit, Lieutenant Viscount Fincastle was awarded the regiment's first Victoria Cross whilst serving with the Malakand Field Force.

In 1900, at the special request of Lord Roberts, the regiment sailed from India to Port Elizabeth for action in the Boer War. The final visit to India in 1937 was terminated, in December 1939, by an order to return to England for mechanisation. The regiment fought in Europe throughout the First World War, and the Second World War found them further afield – in North Africa and later Italy.

After the First World War it was planned to reduce the cavalry by disbanding four regiments. Those chosen were the three junior cavalry regiments, 19th, 20th and 21st and the 5th Royal Irish Lancers. Originally raised in 1689, the 5th had been disbanded in 1799 but reformed in 1858 so its members regarded themselves as amongst the more senior. The decision to disband the 5th caused so much indignation that the matter was raised in Parliament. Eventually, in 1922, the War Office decided against disbandment and the regiments in question were amalgamated, with the 16th/5th The Queen's Lancers coming into being that year. The amalgamated regiment maintains its proud royal association: HM the Queen is its Colonel-in-Chief.

Right: A trooper in marching order, 1891; by J. Charlton.
NATIONAL ARMY MUSEUM, LONDON

Following spread: Charge of the 16th the Queen's Lancers at the Battle of Aliwal, 1846; by T. Harris after H. Martens.
NATIONAL ARMY MUSEUM, LONDON

J. Charlton

The 2nd Punjab Cavalry

The Duke of Wellington aside, only Samuel James Browne, VC, has given his name to a regiment and to a piece of equipment.

In 1858 during the Indian Mutiny, Browne, accompanied by a single trooper, attacked and captured an enemy gun. He was wounded on his knee, and shortly after his left arm was cut off at the shoulder. Thereafter Browne found it hard to manage his sword. It swung loosely from a sling, scraping along the ground as he walked, so he designed a belt which not only kept the sword firmly in place but left the arm free. It also carried a pistol in such a way that the owner would not be injured by an accidental discharge (by no means a rare occurrence then). The Sam Browne belt is still worn today by officers in many foreign forces, as well as by those in the British Army. The original belt can be seen in the National Army Museum, London.

During the action of 1858 Browne commanded the 2nd Punjab Cavalry, an irregular unit he had been ordered to raise in Lahore nine years previously. As the regiment's normal duties were to patrol the Punjab border, the order to go south to help quell the Mutiny was received with considerable excitement. The regiment took part in the assault on Delhi and the relief of Lucknow, and at Agra another of its officers, Dighton Probyn, won the Victoria Cross.

Irregular units were based on the *sillidar* system: the recruit provided his own horse and weapons and in return got a higher rate of pay than those in the regular cavalry. The irregulars were usually dressed and armed in the local style, which was more suitable than European clothing for the duties they were to perform.

After the Mutiny the 2nd Punjab Cavalry returned to their normal frontier-post duties. In 1878 they took part in the expedition to Afghanistan, when the men had to put up with appalling weather and sparse rations. The regimental history states that, in such a climate, the efficiency – indeed the lives – of the horses and ponies depended on their having a full complement of protective covering: none of it could be sacrificed in the interests of speed. Gastronomically, the horses were less demanding. The historian describes a five-day experiment with horse-biscuit tried at Kandahar. It was found that

. . . with grass or *bhusa* a horse could perform hard work with two *seers* of biscuit as well as with double the quantity of grain, and that with four *seers* of biscuit, and no forage whatever, he could efficiently perform hard work for that time without being much reduced in condition.

Until the Mutiny the Army in India was organised in the three entirely separate presidencies of Bengal, Madras and Bombay. When responsibility passed from the East India Company to the Crown in 1861, the armies still retained their individual independence. So, although control of the Punjab Frontier Force was transferred from the civil authority to the Commander-in-Chief in 1886, it was not until 1903 that the Army in India was unified. This involved changes in designation.

The 2nd Punjab Cavalry's application to be known as Sam Browne's Horse was rejected and they became the 22nd Cavalry (Frontier Force). However, the authorities reconsidered the application the following year and the regiment was renamed the 22nd Sam Browne's Cavalry (Frontier Force). Had Sam Browne lived two years longer he would have seen his name thus perpetuated. Promoted general in 1888, and made a Knight Commander of the Star of India in 1876 and a Knight Grand Cross of the Bath in 1891, he died in 1901 at Ryde on the Isle of Wight.

In 1916 the regiment left the Indian frontier again, this time for Mesopotamia. The First World War showed up the defects of the *sillidar* system so, for the sake of efficiency and economy, the existing cavalry regiments were paired in 1921; the 22nd was joined by the 25th Cavalry (Frontier Force), formerly the 5th Punjab Cavalry, and was renamed the 12th Cavalry (Frontier Force). In 1947, when partition between India and Pakistan took place, this regiment was disbanded.

Facing page: Carved figure of a sowar (an Indian trooper), 2nd Punjab Cavalry circa 1885.

Left: General Sir Samuel Browne, VC.

Below: Portraits of the 2nd Punjab Cavalry engraved by T. Harris after W. Fane, published 1856 in the series 'Ackermann: Indian Costumes'.

ALL: NATIONAL ARMY MUSEUM, LONDON

The Boer War

In 1899, 40,000 Boer farmers declared war on the British Empire. They inflicted a series of humiliating reverses on the most experienced regular army of the day.

A strenuous love of independence had first driven the forefathers of the burghers into the wide lands north of the Orange River. This same love led to a first quarrel between Great Britain and Transvaál which had ended so disastrously for Great Britain at Majuba Hill on 27 February 1881, when General Colley was ignominiously defeated and the British had to negotiate a settlement.

The discovery of gold in the Rand and the harsh treatment meted out by President Kruger to the Uitlanders who flocked to Johannesburg to work it, together with the foolish Jameson Raid,

did not help matters and by the summer of 1899 war was inevitable.

It used to be said that every man born in South Africa is a Boer at heart. Certainly any man who went to seek his fortune under the Boer standard was by instinct a soldier and by birthright a trained skirmisher and mounted infantryman who understood the care of horses and needed no training.

In 1881 they had declared their Petition of Rights which clearly stated their position and read:

With confidence we lay our case before the whole world, be it that we conquer or die; liberty shall rise in South Africa like the sun from the morning clouds, like liberty rose in the United States of North America.

little daylight remaining French decided to attack.

The battle area south of the Elandslaagte railway station had the form of a plain surrounded by a horseshoe of hills with the toe to the south. Colonel Hamilton commanded the infantry. With the 15th Dragoon Guards and some 5th Lancers on their left and on the right, the infantry advanced eastwards and soon occupied the western arm of the horseshoe. There was a violent storm and the light was fading fast. After a short artillery bombardment French ordered Hamilton to advance. The attacking forces included the dismounted Imperial Light Horse consisting mainly of Johannesburg men whose failure to go to Jameson's aid had branded them with cowardice and their city with the name of 'Judasburg'. They were out to vindicate their honour. Conditions were made difficult by the drenching rain but the Gordons, Manchesters and Devons together with the Imperial Light Horse, though suffering heavy casualties, spreadeagled the Boers from the hog's-back. The Boers then used their 'white flag' tactics which fooled the British. A party of Boers, during the ceasefire, dashed up the slope and emptied their magazines point blank into the British soldiers crowded on the summit. The Boers drove them off the crest, recaptured the guns and turned them on the Devons, advancing up the hill. The British started to retreat but Hamilton and Sir John French restored the situation.

Meanwhile the 5th Dragoon Guards and 5th Lancers had been waiting concealed near Elandslaagte station. As the Boers passed across their front the order was given to charge. With bared sabres and levelled lances the two squadrons dashed forward and rode over and through the panic-stricken Boers who were severely punished and opened out to try to save themselves by flight. But their little ponies were no match for the big cavalry horses who rode beyond them, rallied and rode back to complete the havoc. The cavalry gave their cloaks to the wounded Boers and General Koch, fatally wounded, was carried back to Ladysmith.

Three Victoria Crosses were won in this action and during the battle the infantry, gunners and cavalry not only combined successfully but also carried out their separate roles to perfection.

Above: 'The Advance to Relieve Kimberley'; a painting by G. D. Giles. NATIONAL ARMY MUSEUM, LONDON

Overleaf: Royal Horse Artillery crossing a pontoon bridge under fire during the Second Boer War, 1900, by George Scott. NATIONAL ARMY MUSEUM, LONDON

Then it will be, from the Zambesi to Simons Bay, Africa for the Afrikanders!

In the same year Mr Gladstone had expressed Britains' position in the matter, saying:

I have always regarded the South African question as the one great unsolved and perhaps insoluble problem of our colonial system.

Before the bulk of the British forces under Buller arrived there was a great deal of fighting in Natal and it is with one of these early battles that we are now concerned. Though small in scale it was a great British victory and there are those who are convinced that had there

been more victories like it early on the war might never have assumed its later proportions.

On 19 October, while commandos were engaged at Talana Hill, General Koch's Levies had moved down the centre of north Natal, reaching the Biggarsberg Mountains. Patrols had advanced south as far as Elandslaagte half-way between Dundee and Ladysmith. They occupied the station and cut rail, road and telegraphic communications. Sir John French moved up from Ladysmith to clear the neighbourhood and restore communications which he soon accomplished, the Boers fleeing to the nearby Kopjes. French decided, however, that he needed reinforcements to clear them completely. These arrived in the afternoon and though there was

The Australian Cavalry at War

If a combination of independence of thought, quickness in decision and boldness in action is what is described as 'the cavalry spirit' then surely Australians must be amongst those who have been most heavily endowed with it. Farmers, sheepmen, cattle-ranchers and jackaroos, accustomed to the great spreads of country and distant horizons, and brought up with horses since their childhood, formed the backbone of the soldiers who answered their country's many calls from the first Maori Wars to the bloody victories of Vietnam.

But although this is the story of cavalry the Australians did not raise units as such, believing that their greatest qualities could only be brought to full flower in what was really a mounted-infantry role. After the Maori Wars in New Zealand, two batteries of artillery, properly horsed, were offered to the British to assist them against the fanatical Mahdi in Khartoum. They left Sydney in 1885, nearly a quarter of a million citizens of the capital giving them a tumultuous farewell. Although they returned in 1886 the first milestone in Australia's military history had been laid.

For the South African War Australia despatched some 6,500 troops and 6,700 horses, all their infantry finally becoming mounted. This provided Lord Roberts with the facility of wide flanking movements which were the determining factor in the relief of Kimberley and the later advances on Bloemfontein and Pretoria. The South African veldt with its great empty plains was a natural backdrop to their activities and suited the Australians with their eye for country and bushcraft. They campaigned for three years leaving South Africa with a reputation for scouting, reconnaissance and rugged fighting second to none.

In these wars they had produced a great officer named Chauvel, who years later in the Sinai Desert in 1916 hoisted his pennant as commander of the Anzac Mounted Division consisting of the Australian Light Horse and the New Zealand Mounted Rifles. When the Turks were threatening the Suez Canal, Chauvel had taken up a position at Romani, twenty-three miles from the Canal, near the sea and surrounded by great sandhills. The 14,000 Turks who attacked Romani were routed, Chauvel proving a master of strategy which later resulted in his promotion to lieutenant-general and command of the Desert Mounted Corps. This force, under Allenby, was planned to drive the Turks out of Palestine in what was to become one of the greatest cavalry campaigns of all history. Allenby had been appointed as Commander-in-Chief to give the command a shake-up and some much needed drive after Murray's abortive attacks on the Turks in Gaza.

In his plans for the advance Allenby was insistent that Beersheba was to be seized on the first day of the column's attack against the Turks. Failure to do this would enable the Turks to re-organise their defences and upset the plan to roll up their line and outflank Gaza. On 27 October 1917 Allenby launched his offensive and the drive on Beersheba. The role of the Australian Light Horse was to be particularly important for they had to sweep round the south and south-east of Beersheba and storm it from the rear.

This was the cavalry role *par excellence* and when their time came they moved off at a trot, the sound of drumming hooves, clinking metal and creaking leather creating a symphony symbolical of a cavalryman's nirvana. Quickening their pace as they rode at the Turkish trenches the thundering mass of men and horses charged into and over the Turks, shooting, bayoneting and demoralising them until the remnants threw down their weapons and begged for mercy.

Beersheba had been secured and the charge of the Australian Light Horse set the standard for the rest of the campaign. Ten months later Jerusalem was captured and Allenby had launched his final attack which diminished the Turkish right flank and began a pursuit ending at Aleppo, five hundred miles to the north.

By 1918 the cavalry force in the area comprised the largest body of mounted troops to be used in modern warfare and the pattern of their actions was set by the Australian Light Horse at Beersheba raising the curtain on what was to be one of the last appearances of horsed cavalry on the modern battle-field.

The Australian's great fighting record was enhanced to undreamt of heights in the Second World War when the vast continental homeland itself was in danger. The march of time, however, had overtaken the horse and though the cavalry spirit remained as a built-in heritage in Australian soldiers, the roll-call in the campaigns in the Western Desert, Malaya, the islands of the Pacific and later, in Korea and Vietnam, did not include the horse.

Right: Detail from 'The Battle of Romani, 4 August 1916,' by G. W. Lambert.
AUSTRALIAN WAR MEMORIAL, CANBERRA

Following spread: 'Light Horse in action east of Jordan – the Es Salt Raid, 30 April 1918', by G. W. Lambert.
AUSTRALIAN WAR MEMORIAL, CANBERRA

G.W. LAMBERT ARA
HON. CAPT. A.I.F.

The Horse in Two World Wars

In 1914, when the British Army was once again plunged into the cockpit of Europe the manual *Cavalry Training* reiterated the fact that 'the moral effect of a mounted attack with sword or lance remains as great as ever'. The charge-in-line was still the pipe-dream of supporters of the *arme blanche*!

The 'weight on horse' problem had still not been solved however, and mounts were burdened with an average twenty-two stone of saddlery, arms and ammunition, equipment and rider. Nearly all artillery was horse-drawn, six horses to each field-gun and eight or twelve to the medium and heavy types.

British yeomanry and cavalry horses numbered 45,000 in 1914 and by 1918 the figure had risen to close upon half a million! The first contact in the war between the British Expeditionary Forces and the Germans came on 22 August 1914 when the 4th Dragoon Guards pushed out two officer patrols from Oburg, north towards Soignies. One of these found a German picquet on the road, fired on it and drove it off.

Unenterprising, the German cavalry were still trained on the principles that had brought them success some forty-four years previously at Rezonville. Dismounting to fight was beneath them and even in the limited mounted action that took place they were unable to better the British and so as early as September 1914, at Compiègne, in what was undoubtedly the first cavalry action of the war, Lt-Col D. G. M. Campbell of the 9th Lancers with thirty men charged a German Squadron, 120 strong, completely overwhelmed it, rallied and withdrew successfully.

But very little shock action could be employed in France and the longer the war lasted the less real cavalry work there was to do and the 'gap' through which they were to surge never materialised.

No less noble, however, were the thousands of draught animals on which the armies were almost entirely dependent for the movement of their guns and the supply of ammunition, rations and all other material. These splendid creatures, truly the work-horses of the armies in the field, suffered more by privation than battle casualties and, like their human masters, endured depredation more dreadful than ever before witnessed in history. The picture 'Goodbye, Old Man', showing a soldier bidding goodbye to his dying mount, poignantly portrays the relationship of man and beast in a war of wholesale massacre of both.

Unlike the Western Front, however, Allenby in his campaign in the Middle East was able to employ his three cavalry divisions to the full and their advance to Aleppo and the crushing defeat of the Turks was a campaign which owed much to the horse.

The Desert Mounted Corps of some 20,000 Australian, New Zealand and Indian cavalry was the largest force of horsemen to operate tactically under one command during war and there are valiant tales of Hobson's Horse, the Sherwood Rangers, Gloucestershire Hussars and the Yeomanry Regiments of Warwick, Worcester, Buckinghamshire and Dorset. By 1919, however, they were all home again in their native shires and once more the reduction of forces began. From then on, with the advance of mechanisation, it was obvious that the armoured fighting vehicle must sooner or later supersede the horse as the cavalryman's mount.

In 1928 the first regular cavalry in Britain, and indeed the whole world, the

11th Hussars and 12th Lancers were converted to armoured car units and by 1938 the process was practically complete. So in 1940 the British Expeditionary Force went to France without a single horse. The French and German armies depended to an enormous extent not only on horse transport but on horsed cavalry. Brigadier Peter Young writes of having seen the leading scouts of the Reconnaissance Company of the 7th German Infantry Division dead in a ditch on the Roubaix-Courtrai road, the legs of their horses sticking up in the air.

Poland was more cavalry minded than any other nation at the outbreak of the war and at that time only three of her forty-one cavalry regiments were mechanised, the horsed strength of the cavalry and supporting horse artillery being 37,000. Hitler's elite SS Corps included

five cavalry divisions, the well-known 'Florian Geyer' (8th SS Division) among them and in 1944 the famous 15th (SS) Cossack Cavalry Corps was formed. The Russians, requiring everything on a colossal scale, employed more than thirty cavalry divisions and were said to have had some 1,200,000 horses serving their cause.

By the end of 1941 only two British cavalry regiments, the Cheshire Yeomanry and the Queen's Own Yorkshire Dragoons, remained mounted. They were mechanised as soon as the French surrendered in Syria and the Cheshire Yeomanry claim to be the last British cavalry regiment to have ridden horses on active service; though in 1943, during the Italian Campaign, the King's Dragoon Guards formed an *ad hoc* troop for mounted patrol work.

In Burma, General Wingate's Chindits and the Special Force units operating behind the Japanese lines depended almost entirely on horse, pony or mule transport for supplies and ammunition. The Japanese also employed large numbers of horses.

Thankfully, horses are no longer being bred and trained to seek their fate on some obscure battlefield, but their legend remains.

Below: 'Greetings at the Crossroads', a watercolour by R. Simpkin.
NATIONAL ARMY MUSEUM, LONDON

Overleaf: 'The Taking of the Guns' by R. Caton Woodville; the 9th Lancers near Mons 1914. ILLUSTRATED LONDON NEWS

Top: British guns going into action: a dash through an old French town, 1917; drawn by F. Matania. SPHERE, 29 DECEMBER 1917

Below: A Stirrup-charge: an incident of Waterloo is repeated at St Quentin in 1914 by the Scots Greys; painting by R. Caton Woodville. ILLUSTRATED LONDON NEWS, 12 SEPTEMBER 1914